MW00465401

Are You the Unchurched?

Are You the Unchurched?

How to Develop an Authentic Relationship with
God inside or outside of Church

Gabrie'l J. Atchison

CASCADE *Books* · Eugene, Oregon

ARE YOU THE UNCHURCHED?
How to Develop an Authentic Relationship with God inside or outside of
Church

Copyright © 2022 Gabrie'l J. Atchison. All rights reserved. Except for brief
quotations in critical publications or reviews, no part of this book may
be reproduced in any manner without prior written permission from the
publisher. Write: Permissions, Wipf and Stock Publishers, 199 W. 8th Ave.,
Suite 3, Eugene, OR 97401.

Cascade Books
An Imprint of Wipf and Stock Publishers
199 W. 8th Ave., Suite 3
Eugene, OR 97401

www.wipfandstock.com

PAPERBACK ISBN: 978-1-6667-1165-3
HARDCOVER ISBN: 978-1-6667-1166-0
EBOOK ISBN: 978-1-6667-1167-7

Cataloguing-in-Publication data:

Names: Atchison, Gabrie'l J.

Title: Are you the unchurched? : how to develop an authentic relationship
with God inside or outside of church / Gabrie'l J. Atchison.

Description: Eugene, OR : Cascade Books, 2022 | Includes bibliographical
references.

Identifiers: ISBN 978-1-6667-1165-3 (paperback) | ISBN 978-1-6667-1166-0
(hardcover) | ISBN 978-1-6667-1167-7 (ebook)

Subjects: LCSH: Christian education. | Secularism. | Church renewal.

Classification: BV1467 .A83 2022 (print) | BV1467 .A83 (ebook)

All scripture quotations are from the New Revised Standard Version
Bible: Catholic Edition, copyright © 1989, 1993 National Council of the
Churches of Christ in the United States of America. Used by permission.
All rights reserved worldwide.

To Dorothy

Table of Contents

Introduction: Are You the Unchurched? | 1

Chapter 1: Radical Self-Acceptance | 15

Chapter 2: Love Your Neighbor | 27

Chapter 3: Love Your God | 39

Chapter 4: If You Experienced Abuse at Church . . . | 54

Appendix A: To Church or Not to Church? . . .
   That Is the Question! | 65

Appendix B: Three Five-Minute Bible Study Lessons | 69

Bibliography | 79

Introduction

Are You the Unchurched?

> One of the teachers of the law came and heard them
> debating. Noticing that Jesus had given them a good an-
> swer, he asked him, "Of all the commandments, which
> is the most important?" "The most important one," an-
> swered Jesus, "is this: 'Hear, O Israel: The Lord our God,
> the Lord is one. Love the Lord your God with all your
> heart and with all your soul and with all your mind and
> with all your strength.' The second is this: 'Love your
> neighbor as yourself.' There is no commandment greater
> than these." (Mark 12: 28–31)

RECENTLY, WE HAVE SEEN several studies about a group of Christians
who have been defined as "the unchurched." Unchurched defines
a group of people who identify as Christian *and* yet have not attended church in more than six months. They are also known in
our community as the "submarine Christians" (so called because
they surface only a few times a year) or "CEOs" (which stands for
Christmas and Easter Only). Other members of this group may
not set foot in any church until a wedding, baby blessing, or funeral draws them in. And these are the people who voice concern
about the church burning down simply because of their presence.

Christian research institutes started to study unchurched
Christians, because the church as an institution is dying.[1] Church-

1. Many of these studies are cited in Kinnaman and Lyons, *UnChristian*,
chs. 1 and 2.

1

es have lower attendance, and as a result, most cannot stay afloat without the offerings and tithes of parishioners. As society changes, the role of formal religion in family life has become less significant. In most parts of the country, people who would still identify as Christians do not attend church on a regular basis. Many young adults have grown disillusioned with the church. In the past, teens and young adults would stop attending church regularly as they began to venture out and learn about the world. However, in the past, those who left church tended to return later as they had children of their own and faced major life challenges. The recent trend is that young people do not return to church, and a new generation of children is growing up without any connection to the church. Whereas some churches can pay insurance, bills, and staff expenses, most are hemorrhaging, trying to keep the doors open for aging parishioners and a handful of families. The purpose of the research on unchurched Christians was to help pastors and other church leaders figure out what to do to attract more people into their churches and to retain their young people.

The purpose of this book is not to save the institution of the church. What drives me is a desire to encourage Christians to find and nurture an authentic relationship with the God of their own understanding. You may find that relationship inside a church or on a park bench, at the beach, or while listening to a song while you are stuck in traffic. What is important is the relationship. *All that is important is your relationship with God!* By strengthening our relationship with God, we are compelled to love ourselves and to love other people as an expression of that love.

Whereas other books have been written *about* the unchurched, I am interested in writing *to* the unchurched. In my search to reach this population, I have found that earlier studies have unearthed some important common characteristics of people who fit into this category. Many unchurched Christians—both young and old—are simply independent thinkers. They are free-spirited individuals who value critical thinking. The rituals and practices of traditional church services do not have meaning to them, and so they find church attendance boring, irrelevant, and a waste of time. Some are adults who were forced to endure church as children, with no context or building of their faith, and therefore stopped attending as soon as they became adults. In many instances, the behavior of other Christians in church was the main factor in driving people away. Churchgoing Christians tend to be described as rigid, judgmental, or hypocritical.

Overwhelmingly, young adults who were studied named hostility towards lesbian, gay, bisexual, transgender, and queer (LGBTQ+) people as the reason they do not attend church. "While most young churchgoers believe that the Bible does not condone homosexuality, their conviction about this is waning, and they are embarrassed by the church's treatment of gays and lesbians."[2] Many heterosexual Christians would prefer a worship space that is open and welcoming to LGBTQ+ Christians, especially when they have family and close friends they would like to invite to church. Many unchurched Christians call themselves "spiritual but not religious," because they cannot find any energy or spirit within the church. And finally, there are among the group those who are survivors of clergy or lay leader sexual abuse, who find church to be a very unsafe space.

The central value identified through interviews with Christians who do not attend church is a desire for connection. They yearn for ways to form community with others with whom they can share a collective sense of purpose. They are looking for fellowship and a space where everyone will be loved and accepted. The studies concluded that churches can reach this population by having special events that bring together church members but are welcoming to all in the community. Churches need to position themselves to serve the needs of people in the community outside of church walls. The church as an institution has fallen short for many in this regard.

Based on my understanding of the research, the unchurched are Christians who are:

2. Kinnaman and Lyons, *UnChristian*, 101.

- College-educated
- Progressive
- Forward-thinking
- Independently minded
- Seeking
- Critically thinking
- Community-oriented
- Generous
- Compassionate

Do you see yourself reflected in these definitions of the unchurched? If you are the unchurched, my goal in this book is to convince you that Christianity, freed from rigid, biblical interpretation, can be dynamic, relevant, and life changing. One set of concepts, relational theology, provides some tools for Christians to connect, or reconnect, with the God of their own understanding. In the next section, I will introduce these concepts as the foundation for my ideas.

Relational Theology as a Path Forward for the Unchurched

Theology frames the way we talk about and think about God and how we form an understanding of God in our lives. Relational theology is a way of thinking and talking about God that places the relationship between humanity and God at the center of Christianity. My goal is to offer you some tools from relational theology to help you connect (or reconnect) with God. These tools can help you find purpose, support, and direction in your life.

Thomas Jay Oord, professor of theology and philosophy at Northwest Nazarene University, has contributed the most to the field of relational theology. In *Relational Theology: An Introduction*, Oord describes relational theology in this way:

> At its core, relational theology affirms two key ideas:
> 1. God affects creatures in various ways. Instead of being
> aloof and detached, God is active and involved in rela-
> tionship with others. God relates to us, and that makes
> an essential difference. 2. Creatures affect God in vari-
> ous ways. While God's nature is unchanging, creatures
> influence the living and loving God, and creation makes
> a difference to God.[3]

The first idea, that "*God affects creatures in various ways,*" loosens up traditional images of God as far above us and in the clouds. In this way, God moves closer and becomes an intimate part of our daily lives. God is a loving entity with whom we can relate. The second part of Oord's assertion, that "*creatures affect God,*" may be harder to accept. Within relational theology, we need God, and God also needs us. For those of us brought up in traditional Christian churches, it may seem wrong and even irreverent to consider our relationship with God as reciprocal. However, I read this idea as a call to action. We are called to continue or complete the work done by Jesus Christ when he was here. "Christ has no body now but yours," Teresa of Ávila stated, "no hands but yours. Yours are the eyes through which must look our Christ's compassion on the world."[4] Our responsibility here is to do as much as we can to al- leviate the suffering of others and to spread the good news of the gospel.

Most importantly, the second part of Oord's assertion means that we matter to God. Each of us is important and special to God. God wants our love, our attention, our gratitude, and our praise. God needs each of us to use our special gifts and talents to enhance humanity and to facilitate a connection between God and as many people as we can touch during our lifetime. We are the body of Christ. We are here to do God's work. In this way, we affect God. Each of us matters to God.

Relational theology encourages us to have a responsible rela- tionship with God based on mutual connection. Oord explains that

3. Thomas Jay Oord, in Montgomery et al., *Relational Theology*, 2.
4. Teresa of Ávila, quoted in Johnson, *Franciscans at Prayer*, 60.

"human beings must be co-laborers with God in the great work of redemption."[5] The relationship between God and humankind is not one of equals and yet can also exist without being abusive or coercive. Many of us find it difficult to relate to God, because we were raised to fear God. If we do have a connection to God, that relationship is based on the belief in a system of punishment and rewards. My friend once told me, "God can squish me like an ant." When I think about it honestly, God has shown up most prevalently when I needed to be brave in a situation, when I needed to show more compassion or love towards others, and when I was crippled with pain or grief. God seems to be on my side. God seems to accept things about me that I am having a difficult time accepting about myself. God seems to be that spirit encouraging me to continue to believe, even when there is no sound reason for my faith. I wonder how my friend can relate to God, when she (at least at some level) believes that God might cause her harm.

There is a Hebrew word, *yare*, which is usually interpreted in the Bible as "fear." Many of us grew up reading texts in the Bible which address fearing God. Another interpretation of that same Hebrew word is "awe." Awe can evoke fear, but mostly the connotations are about being overwhelmed by how amazing something really is. If you have ever stood on the beach and marveled at how large and open it feels and how small you feel in comparison, then you can understand. When you are not on a crowded beach, the sound is almost a vacuum, because it gets swallowed up by the openness and the vastness of the sky and water. If you are on a beach with crashing waves, you can see and hear and feel the power. In our smallness and powerlessness, it may be hard to imagine being important to something so large and so powerful; however, we do matter to God. And that is the beauty in relational theology!

The idea that God is powerful and deserving of our awe, and yet is loving, protecting, and caring, may be difficult to internalize, especially for those of us who grew up with abusive parents or have faced other forms of violence or abuse. Even though we received messages of a loving, protective, and kind God and of Jesus as a

5. Barry L. Callen, in Montgomery et al., *Relational Theology*, 8.

friend in Sunday school, we grew up resolved to endure a relationship that is more distant, judgmental, and punitive. R. Larry
Shelton explains that, in Christ, "we find that salvation is restored
friendship with God."[6] We must return to those foundational
lessons that once brought us so much joy in our lives as young
Christians.

This idea of mutuality is at the core of relational theology.
Two other helpful concepts include understanding God as a living God and experiencing God as love. Honoring and connecting
with a living God brings a sense of immediacy and urgency to our
relationship with God. A living God is equipped to help us manage contemporary concerns and challenges; God is an active par-
ticipant in our lives, and not a removed, detached, and judgmental
being. God relates to what we are going through right now. And,
perhaps most importantly, what we are going through matters to
God. The other helpful concept involves being able to imagine a
God who *is* love. One of the most frequently quoted passages in
the Bible is "For God so loved the world that God gave God's only
son so that who believes in him may not perish but may have eternal life" (John 3:16). The motivation behind the gift of Jesus Christ
is love. Love can be challenging and scary and messy at times, but
it is always good and healing. Love is the motivation and also the
inspiration for our connection with God and with each other. God
always wants what is best for us and wants us to be our best in
relating to others. The concepts of relational theology help us build
authentic and lasting connections with God and with humankind.

Relational Theology Is Based on the Greatest Commandment

There is a story told in two of the Gospels, Matthew 22:37–39
(which I am using for our purposes here) and Mark 12:28–34.
In this story, Jesus is challenged by naysayers and "experts" to
state which commandment is the greatest. In this instance Jesus's

6. R. Larry Shelton, in Montgomery et al., *Relational Theology*, 15.

adherence to the Hebrew Scripture is challenged by others. And Jesus often challenges those in his audience (including us) to consider the spirit as well as the letter of the law. In Matthew, Jesus provides this answer:

> He said to him, "'You shall love the Lord your God with all your heart, and with all your soul, and with all your mind.' This is the greatest and first commandment. And a second is like it: 'You shall love your neighbor as yourself.'" (Matthew 22:37–39)

In the first part of his answer, Jesus quotes portions of the Hebrew Scriptures, about the essence of all law. We have to put God first. In the second part of his answer, Jesus then asks us to love our neighbors (read: all of humankind) as ourselves.

In order to love someone else as you love yourself, the quality of that love must be something worth sharing. For many of us, we have some significant work to do in the area of self-love. In many ways, the journey towards fulfilling the Greatest Commandment begins with radical self-acceptance and love. Additionally, read as a directive, this Scripture can also mean that love for humankind (our neighbors) is *how* we demonstrate our love for God. Reading the Scripture in this way places great importance on how we treat others, our friends and family, coworkers, strangers, and everyone else we encounter on a regular basis. The directive would also inspire greater urgency in our social justice activities, philanthropy, and service work. Then, everything we do for ourselves and others becomes a demonstration or an expression of our love for God.

Why I Think This Might Help You

Relational theology is a set of core principles that may be helpful for you if you are interested in developing an authentic relationship with God. I have found many examples of a relational God in the Bible and also in the stories of inmates, of survivors of violence, and of those in the recovery community. When I learned about relational theology, the concepts resonated with me because

I also understand God to be relational. The path to connection is dynamic and present and yet can often put you at odds with aspects of your own upbringing and traditions. However, the result is a closer relationship with God and with others and a greater sense of purpose in life, for which we all strive.

In studies about the unchurched, researchers uncovered something else I found to be very interesting. Unchurched Christians are also seekers. Based on my having read studies about the unchurched, my guess is that many people who do not attend church regularly are:

- still seeking spirituality
- still looking for direction and purpose in life
- still in need of support when times are hard
- still looking for community

If you are also still searching, having a solid and authentic relationship with God has the potential to help you find that which is missing inside or outside of a church

Relational theology can help you in your search for connection and purpose in many ways. First, by thinking about God relationally, the spiritual experience is not limited to the four walls of the church, nor is it only found in the pages of the Bible. A connection to God can be found in music, dance, literature, a baby's smile, or a beautiful sunrise. All that is required is an openness to the ways in which God is trying to speak to you.

Second, a greater purpose is found when our care of humankind, the earth, and all nonhuman living things becomes an expression of a love for God. Centralizing love of others involves a shift from an exclusive concern for individual salvation to a collective vision of equality and justice. Instead, we dedicate ourselves to making life full and enjoyable for ourselves and others, right now. There is an urgency in faith-based social justice that provides me with a great sense of purpose, as I take responsibility for creating change. I am inspired and encouraged to use my gifts towards a vision of a just and peaceful world.

Third, developing a close relationship with God can also help strengthen your faith for when times are hard. In school, we had fire drills, so we could practice what to do in an emergency. In beginning meditation, we learn to refocus a wandering mind on the breath. In each of these examples, the practice makes us stronger, so when trouble arises, we know what to do and where to focus. Similarly, the relationship with God will help you remember to start with the connection and to start with prayer. With the storm raging around you, you are able to hold on. No matter what the outcome, the comfort comes in knowing that we are all in God's hands. At times, looking at things relationally will encourage you to reach out for help from others. In the same way that your connection with God will make you an advocate for others, there will be times when someone will intercede for you. We are all in this together. Being in relation just helps us to see this more clearly.

Finally, being in relation with God and with humankind will bring you into community with others in ways that you could never imagine. Che Guevara stated, "Let me say, with the risk of seeming ridiculous, that the true revolutionary is guided by strong feelings of love. It is impossible to think of an authentic revolutionary without this quality."[7] Social justice work can be fulfilling and spiritual, and it can also bring you into community with like-minded and passionate people. Under the best circumstances, service can lead to a feeling of community with the very people you are charged to help. Love is contagious! Most of us want to be in community with diverse groups of people from all walks of life. Even though churches can fall short in this respect, we can and do find or create spaces organized around social justice to feel a greater sense of community.

My hope is that this book and, more importantly, the concepts of relational theology will set you on a path towards a stronger connection with God. If you are still looking for purpose, direction, and community, considering a different way of relating with God may help. In full disclosure, I am very much "the churched." I grew up in church and then spent some time away as a young

7. McLaren, *Che Guevara*, 77.

adult. I hit some serious roadblocks when I initially began to look for a place to worship. Now, I identify as queer, and I am as politically left-leaning as you can be as a progressive Christian. I was fortunate to find, over and over again, the kind of church spaces that matched my concept of God and God's love for everyone. Are the people perfect? No. However, I have learned to distinguish their shortcomings and the limitations of institutions from how I feel about Christianity.

My life is the church. I dabble in church history, and I understand how powerful an entity the church has been in American culture. Understanding histories of social change, I recognize how important clergypersons have been in various fights for social justice. I also understand how people can use the Bible and Christianity to cause great harm in the name of God. I am painfully aware of how churches can justify the exclusion of God's children based on sexuality, race, and social class and deny that God has called women to serve as clergy. The church has fallen short in many ways and may indeed be dying as a cultural entity. By some standards, there are more Christians who do not attend church on a regular basis than ones who do. I would argue that we need strong churches now more than ever, but I will not mourn the death of a church that has caused harm. So, I am hoping to help churches change to become what people need in their connection with God. In the meantime, I am hoping that each of us can work to form a relationship with God's people—in the name of God. Again, I am not advocating that you go to church. The impetus is on us, lay leaders and clergy, to make churches into places where you would want to attend. Whatever your future holds, I wrote this book for you to connect or reconnect with God.

What You Will Find in This Book

Are You the Unchurched? introduces relational theology as a tool for Christians who want a closer relationship with God. The foundation of relational theology comes from Jesus's description of the Greatest Commandment—a call to put God first in our lives and to love others as ourselves. Loving others—in the form of intimate connections or the fight for social justice—is how we demonstrate our love for God. One way to be more loving towards others is through love and acceptance of one's self. In chapter 1, I discuss radical self-acceptance—the idea that we are all made in the image of God. Each of us is worthwhile and an important part of the whole (no matter what messages we have received from the past). A love of self becomes the underpinnings for a higher quality of love to show to one's "neighbors."

In chapter 2, I dig deeper into the question of who is one's neighbor. Theologian Carter Heyward describes the connection between people as an energy. We have a choice of using that energy to create a better life for those around us or to do harm and abuse others. Within this context, sin is considered anything that separates you from God—including broken relations. An extension of this love of neighbor is trying to see the other as the self—or as a part of the self. Looking at the connections in our lives in this way makes struggles for social justice more immediate and urgent.

Chapter 3 provides some insight into the relational God of experience and in the Bible. Certain Christian denominations have embraced the idea of the "God of one's understanding." In this chapter, I discuss the God of my understanding and those aspects of my journey that brought me to that understanding. Next, I ask you to consider those spaces where you have encountered God. Who is the God of your understanding? How similar is your personal experience to the concepts of God taught in church or presented in popular culture? The journey towards authentic relationship involves listening to God in new ways and listening and trusting your own experience.

Chapter 4 was written especially for you, if you were a victim of spiritual abuse, ritual abuse, or child sexual abuse at the hands of a lay or ordained church leader. We will never know how many of the unchurched were driven from church spaces because of violence; however, I imagine that these experiences represent a large percentage. If you are a survivor, recognize that you are not alone. Your journey towards trust and intimacy will be extremely challenging, and I hope this chapter can be helpful to you as you heal.

Finally, the appendices of the book provide additional tools, resources, and guidance for you on your path.

1

Radical Self-Acceptance

THERE ARE MANY MESSAGES and lessons attributed to Jesus in the Bible, and many of those are parables and not necessarily straight-forward. However, when asked what is the greatest of all the commandments, Jesus gives an answer that is easy to understand and simple to follow. Jesus tells us to love God and to love our neighbor. Being able to love someone, a neighbor, as yourself implies that you love and treat yourself with kindness and compassion. Take a step back to consider improving the relationship you are having with yourself. How can you love anyone else without a strong connection with yourself? What is the quality of that love you plan to share with others? Radical self-acceptance then becomes the foundation for our connection with other people and with God.

Why Self-Acceptance Is Radical

Self-acceptance is radical because we receive so many messages in this life that we are not good enough and that we are not worth-while. At times, even activities marketed as self-care or self-help start from the premise that something about you needs fixing. Although not a prerequisite for connection with God, self-accep-tance provides a great foundation for the work. You may find more acceptance of self *through* your closer connection with God, and that is fine. However you get there, being better able to accept and love yourself will improve the quality of your connection with God and with others.

Try saying to yourself, "God loves me just the way that I am." What feelings come up for you? Do you feel like you will have to make many changes in your life, before that statement can possibly be true? How do you talk to yourself? How do you treat yourself? Do you feel unacceptable? Do you ask yourself, "Why would God love me?" Is it easier for you to believe the contrary? In this journey, I want you to imagine that God loves you just the way that you are. There are no prerequisites for connection—except maybe your own openness. Imagine that nothing is hidden from God and, further, that you were created by God. You were placed somewhere and have experienced a set of circumstances that have made you who you are. What if there is something about you God can utilize for divine purpose? If it is too early in the process to accept these thoughts, try to keep an open mind. If possible, use a journal on this journey to work through some of the messages you have received that make you believe you are not acceptable as you are. Where do they come from? Are other people the best judge of these facts? As always, be gentle with yourself as you consider these questions. For most of us, self-acceptance is the most difficult hill to climb. However, a relationship with anyone starts with having a good relationship with one's self.

The truth is that we all have intrinsic value. Beyond that, we have gifts and talents to recognize and use to further humanity—a lofty assignment. For the purpose of this discussion, radical self-acceptance can be an important building block in forming relationships with God and humanity. We are all born with the capacity for self-acceptance, and then hardships in life strip away feelings of our own value. Lowered self-confidence can lead to cycles of self-destructive behaviors and the abuse and violation of others. The process of connection with yourself will not be an easy one; however, capacity will deepen with patience and time.

My journey

I feel a little bold writing about self-acceptance when it is something with which I struggle quite regularly. Fortunately, for you and for me, self-acceptance does not have to be accomplished before forming a relationship with God. I find that I have good moments more and more often. The better I feel about myself, the easier it becomes to accept others. And at times, the process of accepting others helped me to accept myself. The source of my inability to see myself clearly is my broken relationship with my father, although not exclusively. Through his abusive behavior, emotional distancing, and abandonment of the family unit, I gained a message that I was unworthy of love, attention, or care. The message was compounded with the behavior of his extended family, teachers with low expectations, and a society unable to welcome or celebrate a bright and sensitive young black girl.

Occasionally, I would experience connection or receive messages of love and affirmation; however, the positive messages were tuned out by the original negative ones. Another set of messages that were difficult to overcome were the ones that were planted by my experiences of sexual abuse and assault as a young person. My father's physical and sexual abuse of me made me feel isolated and out of control of my own body. However, the most difficult part was walking into preadolescence and adolescence believing myself to be an object. I did not have proper boundaries and experienced additional groping and sexual assault by others as a teen. I felt helpless and worthless. I have come to believe that the childhood abuse set me up for this later heartache.

As a young person, I learned not to share the pain I felt—about anything—with others and to wear a mask. Being overweight allowed me the feelings of control I longed to have. A large body made me feel physically safe and invisible at the same time. Emotional eating gave me the comfort I craved. Masks are great coping mechanisms; however, we have to take them off in order to form authentic connections with others. Throughout my life, I would do well until I tried to lose weight or tried to make new friends. I derailed most of my own weight-loss efforts, because the discomfort around facing my fears was too much to bear. I have resolved the struggles I once had with myself around weight; however, intimacy, trust, and connection remain a challenge.

During my process of healing and forgiveness, I came to feel deeply saddened about the broken relationship with my father. I had come to believe that someone or some set of circumstances had broken him as a boy and made him into someone with no capacity for love. By the time my sisters and I met him as an adult, all he could see was what was wrong with all of us. Everything about our unique personalities was wrong. As we grew up, none of our successes mattered to him. This was a profound loss for him. My father had five children before he died, and he did not get to know any of us. He missed out on all the opportunities offered in life to turn things around, mend relationships, or make things better. I feel sad for him. And I spend my life loving as big as I can, in honor of him.

When I was a teenager, someone said to me, "Even a broken clock is right twice a day!" Seemingly, out of the blue, a seed was planted that maybe everything I do is not wrong. Maybe some of the things I do or some of the things about me are right! Perhaps the people around me just are not that good at telling me so. I would have a long journey from those initial thoughts to significant movement on healing and forgiveness, but that simple thought was where it all began.

At times, healing can happen through our efforts to help others. Ernest Hemingway stated, "The world breaks everyone and afterward many are strong at the broken places."[1] Still broken from my childhood trauma, I worked to heal survivors of rape and childhood abuse. My path started when I was in graduate school in Philadelphia. I attended a massive National Organization for Women (NOW) rally in Washington, DC, and wandered into an exhibit of the Clothesline Project. The Clothesline Project allows survivors of violence to express themselves by writing their message on a shirt and then hanging it on a clothesline. Each of

1. Hemingway, *Farewell to Arms*, 226.

the colors represents a different form of violence. Red, pink, and orange were for survivors of rape and sexual abuse; blue or green for incest; and purple or lavender for people attacked due to their sexual orientation. White shirts represented women who had died from domestic violence. By displaying these colorful testimonies, survivors can resist the rebuke of "airing dirty laundry" and not feel so isolated in their pain. I had seen a Clothesline Project exhibit before, but this one was massive. Something profound happened to me as I bore witness to the pain of others. This was a visual affirmation that I was not alone.

I was so caught up in the exhibit that I lost track of time. I was that one on the bus trip who delayed the departure time for everyone else. I was lucky they did not leave me in Washington, DC. I returned to my dorm determined to take my own life. I had one of those two a.m. phone calls with my sister, and she helped me change my mind. I would be back in that dark place many times, and every time, I lived to see another day.

My journey to become strong at my broken places started with my efforts to help others. Still somewhat unable to delve into my specific trauma, I became a strong voice against domestic violence. By the time I entered my thirties, I was a writer/activist/artist living in Boston, lending my energy to different feminist initiatives. I started support groups and participated in local and national protests and events. Later, while living in the Washington, DC area, I decided to become a rape crisis counselor for the organization Rape Abuse and Incest National Network (RAINN). I was not sure if I could handle being that close to my own trauma. I told myself, if I could make it through the orientation, that was my sign that I was far enough along in my own process to do the work. Eventually, I served as a volunteer for one full year. To date, the few hours a week that I spent talking to people in crisis were some of the hardest moments of my life. Through that experience, I became bolder, more confident, and more determined to change society.

During my process of healing, alongside my work with others, I began to journal and seek out other tools for healing. I became better at setting boundaries with people who habitually ignored what I asked of them. I began to believe that I could use my voice to defend myself and that I could remove my mask and talk to others about how I really feel. I worked on getting stronger physically, so I could feel safe. I even took a class in self-defense. Sometimes I worked on these issues with a therapist or in small groups and sometimes on my own. People often say, "Put yourself first!" At that time, not only was I not first on my list of priorities, I was not on the list at all! Now, I am a priority. I am still not quite first, but I am making progress.

When my father died, I told myself I was attending his funeral only for my sisters. But now I am very glad I attended, as that one act became an important part of my healing process. By the time my father died, I had forgiven him. What remained were deep feelings of guilt. When I was a teenager, my father started a new family, and I had a strong belief that he would harm his other children, my stepsiblings. However, I never felt like I was in a position to prove anything or to convince anyone. I had been holding on to that regret. When my father died, I had a complex feeling of grief mixed with relief. At the funeral, I was moved by the true anguish on the part of my half-brother and his young, male cousins on his mother's side of the family. They loved him, and their grief was not mixed. I wondered if my father was capable of loving male children in a way that he could not love my sisters and myself. The situation made me feel hopeful that maybe my father had felt connected to someone in his relatively short life. Maybe he had not harmed other children. And, for the first time, I thought that the situation was not mine to change or control. I was able to release the guilt and the pain of the past, just by witnessing the outpouring of love by the young men. That my father was loved made me feel deserving of love as well.

I tell my story because I am still in process. In many ways, the love I give others is stellar, yet I am still somewhat selfish. I am still holding back by not letting others in. Being vulnerable with others is my challenge. My love for God feels solid, and yet, I feel God encouraging me to connect and be more authentic in my relationships with others. I am compassionate with others but often not with myself. I wanted to tell my story, just in case there are aspects of my story that resonate with your own.

Radical Self-Acceptance

Self-acceptance is often hindered by experiences outside of our control. Some of the roadblocks we face include childhood sexual abuse, neglect, and sexual assault. Experiences of discrimination based on race, gender, sexuality, class, or physical ability can damage our ability to feel acceptable. These experiences may turn inward and manifest as depression or self-loathing. Self-blame and disavowal are coping mechanisms that protect victims from feeling helpless. Messages that say "something must be wrong with me" or "I must have done something to bring this about" can sometimes be easier to manage than accepting the capricious nature of some forms of violence. We may also feel a need to protect the memory or character of our abusers, even within our own heads. In many ways, we can minimize or excuse the behavior of others.

I want a dime for each time I have heard, "Well, if my parents did not love me, then why would anyone else love me?" If you take a step back and examine the lives of your parents, you can begin to see your parents simply as people. They may have been broken early in life. They may have been experiencing mental health or substance abuse struggles. Or, they may have been unprepared or incapable of giving you the love and attention you needed. Your parents may or may not have been at their best as a parent to you. What they felt or were capable of showing cannot be the measure of your sense of self-worth. They may not be the best judge of your character. They may not even know who you really are. Plenty of people have loved you and can love you. And some of these people will be able to express their love in words and in deeds.

Another major roadblock to self-acceptance is that we live in a society that tells us we are unacceptable on a daily basis. Our media preys on our insecurities by convincing us that we are unacceptable so that we will spend money on products that will make us feel better. There are billions of dollars being spent on advertising designed to let us know that we are too old, too fat, too ugly, too bald, etc. We spend our lives being bombarded by messages demanding that we measure up to unattainable standards.

Other people can tear away at your confidence, especially close and intimate friends and family members. Always remember, the way people talk to you is how they talk to themselves on the inside. Often other people will project on to you their own feelings of inadequacy, insecurity, and fear. In the 1990s, there was a popular song called "O. P. P."[2] I am borrowing that acronym to talk about OPP or "Other People's Projections." People, especially those who learned to hide their vulnerability in their youth, have a challenging time dealing with insecurity, fear, or any other strong emotions. They can often project on to you the emotions they are feeling inside. The tough part about dealing with these people is that, most of the time, they are simply not even aware or in touch with what is going on for real. Engaging with such people makes me appreciate hanging out with dogs. Dogs telegraph their intentions before they act—every time. The tense body language of "I am going to chase that squirrel!" is the same each time. Shame on me if I miss it and am dragged across the backyard. People are different because we can feel one thing and say another. The next time someone unloads on you for no reason, take a deep breath and remember that they are down with OPP.

Finally, our messages about being unacceptable may come from church or our religious upbringing. Most Christian education and Sunday school lessons focus on Jesus as our friend. We sing songs and attend puppet shows about positive and uplifting stories from the Bible. However, by the time we are teenagers in the church, God has become a harsh, all-knowing judge who holds us in a general disdain. We get the message that God is watching and does not like who you have become. Another indirect message comes from the church and also from a perception of what Christianity is in society. The idea is that, in order to be a Christian, you have to be perfect or strive for perfection. Many people believe

2. Naughty by Nature, "O. P. P."

that there are certain criteria that need to be met before you are worthy of God's love. The Bible discusses belief (John 3:16), love (Matthew 27:37–39), mercy (Hosea 6:6), and humility (Micah 6:8) as requirements. If you are able to meet those requirements in your imperfection, then that is okay. Most of us do. The quest for perfection in order to deserve love from God sets up another unattainable standard that may make you feel inadequate. And perfectionism is not a good use of your energy.

For LGBTQ+ Christians, a strong message of rejection has caused great harm to individuals and to the church as an institution, as young adults, in general, yearn for inclusive worship spaces. Increasingly, there are "welcoming and affirming" congregations; however, most churches have an implicit "Don't ask, don't tell!" policy, or openly condemn homosexuality from the pulpit. Most LGBTQ+ Christians have had to leave the church or hide who they are in religious spaces. Other people have painful experiences with being exorcized, abused, or humiliated in church or being expelled from the church altogether. Parents of LGBTQ+ or even children who are questioning their own sexuality are put into a bind when they are made to feel like understanding or compassion means that they condone what the church has forbidden. LGBTQ+ youth are overrrepesented among statistics related to teen suicide and homelessness,[3] and the church plays a pivotal role in maintaining this intolerance in society. When LGBTQ+ Christians are pushed out or decide to leave the church, the rejection can have a significant impact on their sense of self.

Back when cassette tapes and the Sony Walkman were popular forms of entertainment, people in the self-help world used to talk about "replacing old tapes." The old tapes are those messages that are given to us by other people about our worth, which we begin to internalize. Later on in life we dredge up these old messages to put ourselves down. Recording new messages includes discovering what you absolutely love about being yourself. You can use affirmations or positive statements about where you are or where you would like to be. Building self-efficacy may also be

3. "Research Brief"; Siciliano, "Religious Rejection."

a way to build self-acceptance. You can build self-efficacy by find-ing something you would like to change about yourself or your environment, marking the changes and celebrating your successes. I learned how to drive when I was in my thirties. As a child and young adult, I never thought I would be able to drive or own a car. I opted out of driver's education in high school and spent a lot of time on Greyhound buses. Now, as I drive along the highway, I can still remember what it felt like to be scared to drive ten miles per hour. I failed the first time I took the driving test, and so it felt so amazing to practice parallel parking on a hill (which is an impor-tant aspect of driving in Massachusetts) and pass the second time. I remember what it felt like to drive my first car for the first time. I try to remember all these moments now as I try to learn how to play the piano. Releasing the need for perfection and celebrating the smallest of victories have made the process very enjoyable.

Another way to create more positive messages for yourself is by being compassionate towards someone else. Some people are challenging to love. When you can push past a difficult personality and love someone who needs love, that's the best way to access self-acceptance. Through the acceptance of others, you may create more space for grace inside of you. Being vulnerable with others while also maintaining your boundaries can be a difficult balanc-ing act. However, both aspects within a relationship are important in building true connection.

Seeing Ourselves the Way God Sees Us

This is a simple prayer for you: "God is for me. God is with me."

One of the strongest arguments that can be made for self-love and self-acceptance is in the recognition that God loves us just the way we are. The path to radical self-acceptance can also include seeing ourselves the way God sees us. In the first chapter of Gen-esis, God creates humankind in God's own image. Being created in the image of God is strong evidence of the unique and special relationship between God and humankind. There are actually two versions of the creation story for human beings. The version in the second chapter, a story of Eve being created from the rib of Adam, is the one with which most of us are familiar. In the version from the first chapter, God, almost at the end of a seven-day process of creation—the heavens, the earth, all of nature, and a diverse array of animals—creates humankind. Many versions of the Bible translate this passage as "Let *us* make humankind in *our* image," because the Hebrew words are plural. The one phrase opens the possibility of inclusion. The image of God is expansive enough to include all of our diversity. This is one of many Bible passages that demonstrate the love of God for humankind. Perhaps the most poignant are found in the stories about Jesus Christ, whose name Immanuel means "God with us!" When read from the perspective of relational theology, the Bible portrays God yearning for connection with God's creation.

In Judaism, *b'tzelem Elohim* ("in the image of God") is foundational to the Jewish value system.[4] This concept bonds us to God and each other and solidifies our commitment to care for all creation. In Genesis, God creates all the other living things; however, it is only humankind that is created in God's image. We can relate to God because we are part of God's self; nothing else in creation holds that distinction. *B'tzelem Elohim* provides a source for self-esteem and an additional commitment to care for all of God's creation in partnership with God.

In addition to being created in God's image, we can also believe that God made us the way we are on purpose. Each of us is a worthwhile and important part of God's creation. Scripture passages in Isaiah (44:2, 64:8) and in Psalms (139:13–18) point specifically to God having a hand in our creation. The psalmist says, "I am fearfully and wonderfully made" (Psalm 139:14). This is our affirmation that not only are we made in the image of God, but we were also formed with great care and intention. In 1 Corinthians 12, we learn that all of us together make up the body of Christ. Although we are many, we are one. Further, each of us has been

4. Wechter, "B'tzelem Elohim."

given a gift. No person should believe that her gift is more valuable than the gift of another. And no one should feel left out, because all of us are necessary. All of Scripture points to a relational God who accepts and loves us as we are. There is indeed a Creator who made us specifically the way we are for the task that we are here to accomplish. Being made in the image of God can help us feel connected to God, to see ourselves as siblings in Christ, and to inspire us to be bold in our efforts to bring justice into this world.

Self-acceptance can be bolstered by seeing yourself the way God sees you. And you are so loved by God. In some ways, internalizing that you are loved can help you understand your worth— even when you are being undervalued by others. God sees you as you really are, and God loves and accepts what God sees in you. Even if you can never understand *why* God loves you, understand *that God loves you!* Second, understand that God made you exactly the way that you are. God needs you to do something very specific that only you can do in furtherance of God's vision—also described as the kingdom (or kin-dom) of God. Third, see yourself as not only intentionally made, loved, and accepted, but also as a very important part of the whole. God sees us as one, even though we spend all of our energy trying to break off into separate groups, identities, and sects. Some people in your life will spend their energy trying to bring you down, because that is the only way they can feel elevated. The truth is that we are all necessary and important. In the next chapter, I address the concept of interdependence in ecological theologies. These concepts include God seeing not only all people as one but also all living things and all of nature as part of the whole. We all need each other. And all of us need you.

2

Love Your Neighbor

IN CHAPTER 1, WE explored the concept of radical self-acceptance as a way to enhance the quality of the love we show to others. Even though I am using the idea of a path to explain the components of relational theology, understand that there is no right or wrong way to relate to God. You may open your heart to social justice issues and to God and find that self-love is a wonderful by-product of those experiences. The relationship is the goal, and what I am outlining in this book can hopefully give you some things to consider along the way.

In this chapter, we will explore the notions of being a neighbor and loving one's neighbors. Within relational theology, we are invited into a process of responsible relationship with God. We work together with God to protect the vulnerable and to care for other people, animals, nature, and the earth. In other words, one's neighbors become all of God's creation. As we begin to see this love and care as our responsibility, we can develop a stronger sense of purpose in life. Social justice work then begins to bring us in community with others. And we can consider our work an expression of our love for God.

Who Is the Neighbor?

In Matthew 27, Jesus explains that second to the Greatest Commandment is the edict to love your neighbor as yourself. As we read this passage, we are left to ask, "Who is our neighbor?"

In the parable of the good Samaritan (Luke 10:25–37), a law expert asks Jesus what he must do to inherit eternal life. Jesus provides an answer similar to the Greatest Commandment in Matthew 27. He says, "Love the Lord your God with all your heart and with all your soul and with all your strength and with all your mind, and, love your neighbor as yourself." Then, the law expert asks Jesus, "And who is my neighbor?" At this point, Jesus tells the story of the good Samaritan. In the story, the good Samaritan is the one who cared for a man who had been beaten down and robbed, when others would not stop to help. In many ways, the Samaritan went above and beyond to care for a stranger, with no apparent gain for his actions. Jesus asks the law expert, "Which of these three do you think was a neighbor to the man who fell into the hands of robbers?" The expert in the law replied, "The one who had mercy on him." Jesus told him, "Go and do likewise" (Luke 10:36–37).

The neighbor is every person, especially those in need. In Matthew 25:31–46, Jesus provides more insight into this idea in his parable about separating the sheep from the goats. In this parable, Jesus explains that righteousness involves providing for the needs of the hungry, the thirsty, and the naked; inviting in the stranger; and visiting the sick and those in prison. Jesus explains that when you care for "the least of these," you are caring for him. In these two stories, being a neighbor is a quality to which we should aspire. We are imbued with the responsibility to share God's love, care, and concern with the most vulnerable. Jesus is very firm about the distinction between people who take these responsibilities to heart and those who do not. At the end of the parable, Jesus says that those who do not care for others "will go away to eternal punishment, but the righteous to eternal life" (Matthew 25:46).

Power in Relation

Loving one's neighbor is a central facet of relational theology, because we can create more authentic and intimate connections with each other as an expression of love for God. Carter Heyward describes that connection between us as an energy or *power in relation*. In life, we have the choice of using this power to heal and enact social justice or to abuse people and cause great harm. Feminists once discussed this distinction as "power over" others in contrast to "power with" others. Power in relation involves the energy and monumental change that can happen when people connect and work together to bring about change.

In *The Redemption of God: A Theology of Mutual Relation*, Carter Heyward distinguishes between *exousia* and *dunamis* forms of power. *Exousia* is power or authority given through "official social legitimation,"[1] whereas *dunamis* is a raw and spontaneous power unregulated by outside factors. Jesus operated under a seemingly self-appointed authority, which seemed dangerous to those in positions of power. The *dunamis* is the power in relation that can be shared between people through intimacy (or touch) and through the ability to bear the pain of others without looking away. For Heyward, our purpose here is to be in right relation with God. Together, in co-creation with God, we become responsible for creating the just world that we all desire.[2] She adds that many shy away from this power out of fear.

In *Jesus and the Disinherited*, Howard Thurman, inspired by the way that Jesus negotiated his *dunamis* power, applied lessons of power in relation to his message for African American people. Howard Thurman wrote his seminal book during the 1930s, when African Americans in northern cities lived in horrible conditions and experienced regular abuse and discrimination from white Americans and the police. Families moved from the South for job opportunities and to escape lynching, only to find additional horrors in the North. Before the civil rights movement of the 1950s

1. Heyward, *Redemption of God*, 3.
2. Heyward, *Redemption of God*, 3.

and 1960s, there often was no legal recourse for the pain they experienced. In his book, Thurman asks if Jesus could be relevant to a group of people "whose backs were against the wall."[3] He wonders if a message of love and forgiveness could speak to people experiencing the capricious nature of racial terrorism.

In most situations, white people were sanctioned by law and custom to wield power over black life. Thurman appeals to black people who were tempted to use the defensive coping mechanisms of deception, hate, or fear. Rather, he asks them to focus on love. Thurman's argument is that coping strategies would serve as short-term solutions and would lead to more harm. Facing hatred with love, for Thurman, would be the only way to form an authentic connection with humankind and with God. Thurman asks African Americans to tap into a deep well of humility. When a person is not able to be controlled or destroyed through humiliation, some of her power can return to her. He explains that forgiveness can happen only when the person without power begins to see herself as an equal to those in power. The disempowered or the disinherited can then become "freed souls," who have the inner strength to thrive, love, and live in their fullness—in spite of their circumstances.

Liberation theologies often ask us to consider Jesus Christ in his own context while also understanding him as a unique combination of human and divine. Jesus the man, in his context, belonged to an ethnic minority group living under the authority of a powerful military force. Read with an understanding of Jesus in his context, Jesus's words about humility, forgiveness, and love of one's enemy present a strategy for people without access to formal power. Jesus inspires the nurturing of an inner strength to withstand things outside of our control. Confident and courageous, we are guided by a vision of peace and improved conditions not just for ourselves but for future generations and others in our community. Power in relation provides us with the space to welcome even those causing harm back into the circle.

3. Thurman, *Jesus and the Disinherited*, 13.

Power in relation then becomes a choice. The same power can be used to connect and heal or to abuse and harm. There are times when we are not part of the power structure, nor are we experiencing the impact of discrimination or abuse in a direct way. These are the times when our job is twofold. We need to provide direct care to those in need, while also working to encourage those in power to change their ways. This encouragement may come in the form of using leverage to persuade, nonviolent political action, or economic divestment.

One helpful concept from ecological and ecofeminist theologies is interdependence. Interdependence becomes the motivating factor for power in relation. In a world focused on capitalism, militarism, and individuality, Indigenous people and other people of color, poor people, and women are often not valued outside their roles as servants. Vulnerable people and nature are similarly treated as resources that can be used, exploited, and discarded. Theologians posit that similar attitudes that lead to sexism, racism, and class exploitation cause us to have a blatant disregard for how we relate to nature. Various passages in the Bible are used to support the domination of nature by humankind and the subjugation of women by men, which adds another layer to the challenge of creating change.

The concept of interdependence challenges us to see ourselves as connected to each other and to all living things. We can begin to see ourselves as stewards of nature and caretakers of the earth. Each aspect of the ecosystem is valued, respected, and an important part of the whole. Interdependence brings us back to the Greatest Commandment by showing us that our neighbor is everyone, and we should also extend our respect and care to all living things. We all need each other. You should love your neighbor because you need your neighbor and your neighbor needs you! Being able to see things in this way breaks up the need for hierarchy. We can live in harmony with each other and with the earth.

Finally, one of the best examples of power in relation happens when someone who survives a great tragedy or trauma dedicates his life to helping others going through the same thing. One story of power in relation is told by Karen Baker-Fletcher in her book *Dancing with God*. Baker-Fletcher discusses Mamie Till, the mother of Emmett Till, who was lynched in 1955. Emmett Till was a fourteen-year-old boy who lived in Chicago and traveled to Mississippi to visit his family. During his visit, he was falsely accused of whistling at a white woman in a store. That night, a racist mob beat Till, shot him in the face, and threw his body into the Tallahatchie River. During that era, lynching was a crime for which very few perpetrators were held accountable. In spite of her grief, Mamie Till held an open-casket funeral. The image of Emmett Till's battered and mutilated body moved through the black press. The funeral for Till became the catalyst for many people who became leaders in the movement for civil rights. Seeing that image was the moment they decided to join the fight. Rosa Parks explained, four months after her decision to stay seated on the bus, "I thought of Emmett Till, and when the bus driver ordered me to move to the back, I just couldn't move."[4] We know Emmett Till's name, because his mother fought to keep this story in the forefront of the country's consciousness. In 2017, the woman who accused Emmett Till of acting inappropriately recanted her story.[5]

One contemporary example of power in relation is found in the testimony of Rachel Lloyd, founder of Girls Educational and Mentoring Services (GEMS), an organization in Harlem, New York, serving girls who have been victims of sex trafficking. Lloyd, who was born in England, was prostituted when she moved to Germany as a young adult. She found her way out of the life and relocated to New York City to work with women in prison. With very few resources, Rachel Lloyd started GEMS when she realized how young girls were when they were being forced and coerced into prostitution. There was also a need to help law enforcement and society see these girls as victims rather than as criminals.

GEMS deals with the psychological and emotional aspects of being drawn into the commercial sex industry at such a young age by addressing the trauma experienced by girls at home and on the streets. And the organization's unique stance comes from having a

3. Carrier, "Traveling the Civil Rights Trail," para. 11.

4. Pérez-Peña, "Woman Linked."

founder who understands from personal experience what the girls are going through. Rachel Lloyd and other survivors worked to get police departments and criminal justice agencies to redirect girls to resources as alternatives to prison. Members of the organization also advocated on the national level to change the definition of trafficking to include any commercial sex activity involving people under eighteen. Once young people being exploited were characterized as trafficking victims, they could receive resources and support from the federal government. More importantly, they could be seen as children in need of care by society and by law enforcement.

Power in relation, based in the understanding that we are all in this together, gives us the courage to be agents of change. When we work collaboratively, we become co-creators or collaborators with God to transform our communities, the laws in our country, or the way the world perceives an issue. Power in relation in its deepest expression happens when people transform their personal pain into freedom or healing for others. Like Rachel Lloyd, many survivors of sex trafficking have started their own organizations to help women and girls or served in other ways to help other victims. I have found examples of this transformative vision in anti-violence criminal justice, economic justice, and education reform efforts. Many of the mothers of victims of contemporary police brutality and gun violence are at the forefront of campaigns to raise awareness and make change. We are at our best when we use our "power with" in connection with God; we work to undo the damage caused by those who would use "power over" to abuse others.

The Act of Love

What about When Someone Is Difficult to Love?

"Those who say, 'I love God,' and hate their brothers or sisters, are liars; for those who do not love a brother or sister whom they have seen, cannot love God whom they have not seen. The commandment we have from him is this: those who love God must love their brothers and sisters also." (1 John 4:20–21)

"You have heard that it was said, 'You shall love your neighbor and hate your enemy.' But I say to you, love your enemies and pray for those who persecute you. . . . For if you love those who love you, what reward do you have?" (Matthew 5:43–44, 46a)

Love for everyone is aspirational. There are times when your family members or the people within your closest circles are the ones who are the most challenging to love. One thing to remember is that people often reflect back on to you how they are feeling about themselves. Compassion enters the situation when you recognize their behavior as an expression of deep insecurity and pain. People who are the hardest to love are people who are having the hardest time accepting themselves.

Often times challenging people find their way into our churches and single-handedly work to repel as many people as possible from the worship space. I continue to be surprised by how mean people who profess to be Christian tend to be. Christians are mean because they are frustrated. The dichotomy of good/evil and reward/punishment is not a very satisfying way to live. The paradigm falls apart as soon as "bad people" seem to receive favor (or are at least not openly punished). I have concluded that on an institutional level, churches have done a poor job in explaining and demonstrating the grace of God to parishioners. Christians who do not understand God's grace may have a hard time extending grace to themselves and to others. They set unrealistic standards for their own lives and become frustrated with themselves as they fall short. And they take out their frustration on you, when you visit the church for the first time, and accidently sit in "their pew."

Whereas I have great respect for Christian evangelism, sometimes the heavy recruitment of people who do not have a strong foundation is a set-up for disappointment. In Matthew 13:1–9, the parable of the sower, Jesus talks about a sower throwing seeds on the ground along his path. Some seeds were eaten by birds, fell on rocky ground, or were scorched by the sun and could not grow. Others fell among the thorns and could not thrive. Jesus asks us to be like the good soil that brings forth good grain. In his explanation of the parable, Jesus says, "As for what was sown on rocky ground, this is the one who hears the word and immediately receives it with joy; yet such a person has no root, but endures only for a while, and when trouble or persecution arises on account of the word, that person immediately falls away" (Matthew 13:20–21). People who recruit lots of others to Christianity may be indeed throwing seeds on rocky ground. At times, those bringing people into the church make them a promise with expectations that are unrealistic. Newcomers are made to believe if they just follow all the rules, everything in their lives will work out exactly as they want. Recruiters promise a life in Jesus where you will be happy all the time. Often when life gets hard, people will tell you your faith isn't strong enough; that's why things didn't work out. When something catastrophic happens, some people haven't built up a strong enough spiritual foundation to get through it. Their faith falls away.

Under the best of circumstances, opening yourself up for love is risky and challenging. If we are right to believe that we can demonstrate our love for God by loving other people, then extending love to challenging people can become a worthwhile endeavor.

Releasing Past Hurts

Forgiveness is a fundamental aspect of love of neighbor. For the purposes of this discussion, I want to reframe this process as releasing rather than forgiving. Holding on to past hurts is exhausting. Someone who has hurt you has given the burden to you to hold on to for a lifetime. Give the burden back to them. Releasing does not mean that you condone what happened, and it does not involve the other person at all; the process is very personal. In situations where the abuse continues, it is not appropriate to focus on forgiveness. What they are doing has to stop, or you have to get away before trying to work on this process. You also need to be patient with yourself and allow for time to move through the pain without judgment, being compassionate first and foremost with yourself. One can imagine that there is nothing that was done to you in the past that you cannot forgive with time.

Similarly, if you are having trouble forgiving yourself, remember that there is nothing outside of God's grace. In other words, there is nothing so horrible that God cannot forgive you. Behavior that harms you or harms others will need to change. Ask God for help. In the meantime, understanding that you are forgiven removes the shame and self-loathing that can often keep you stuck in self-loathing. I have spent the greater part of my adult life working hard to forgive others, only to find myself stuck when I tried to forgive myself. In reviewing my list of "crimes," I found that there was not one thing for which I couldn't find compassion in another person's testimony. More importantly, I recognized how much I had been punishing myself while in this space of pain by overeating to the point of pain, sabotaging my own efforts to get healthier, and revisiting old trauma by putting myself in dangerous situations.

The same compassion and care I show for others, I had to turn inward. A lot of the challenges were around unprocessed grief and loss. I carried pain that I did not allow myself or could not afford to feel. At the time, grief came out in the forms of low self-confidence and self-loathing. Releasing involves reframing huge chunks of the past as "learning" and as opportunities to get things right. After I lost someone who meant the world to me, I wondered, "Did I show her enough love?" I cannot go back, so I try my best to love others fully and freely.

For some reason, many people have come to believe in a set of prerequisites for God's love and God's grace. They believe that God will love us only if we are loving, and God will forgive us only if we forgive others. I hear something a little different in the Gospels. We are free to love others, because we are loved by God. We are free to forgive others, because we are forgiven by God. Grace has been extended to us, because Christ laid down his body for all of us. Now, we are free to extend that grace to each other. So, love someone who is difficult to love, even if that someone is you!

Seeing the Other as Part of the Self

Once you begin to experience the love of neighbor and see this action as a way to honor and love God, the impetus to work on behalf of justice becomes more immediate. Returning to the Scripture in Matthew 25, Jesus teaches us that when you encounter the least of these, you encounter me. In other words, if you truly care for me, you will care for my people. There is a special concern for those who are among the most vulnerable. This is important, because it outlines how God will be able to care for us all with our help. We become God's instruments for compassion.

Read relationally, this Scripture demonstrates a connection between us all. If someone else's child's school is under-resourced for example, I should be as concerned about it as if my child attends that school. If I meet up with a homeless man, I should imagine that man as my father. And I should have the same level of urgency to help him that I would if I found my father living on the street. Every year during Holy Week, we are invited to experience Jesus's torture and death on the cross. Similarly, we are invited to experience the violence and abuse of other people as our own.

The next step from seeing other people's suffering as our own concern, because we are connected to each other, is seeing other people's suffering as if it were our own. This level of intimacy is transformative and radical. Every time we hear about someone being held in solitary confinement we imagine ourselves in solitary confinement, releasing judgment and imagining how we might feel in solitary confinement. What level of energy, excitement and urgency would I feel about being free? Can I bring that same energy to my work around social justice? Miroslav Volf defines this as making space for the other in the self:

> To describe the process of "welcoming," I employed the metaphor of "embrace." . . . The most basic thought that [the metaphor] seems to express is the will to give

ourselves to others and "welcome" them, to readjust our
identities to make space for them, is prior to any judgment about others, except that of identifying them in
their humanity.[6]

Many Christian traditions emphasize individual salvation to
the exclusion of more communal or collective concerns. The narrow focus on heaven/hell and good/bad leaves little room for the
beautifully messy daily experiment of living, making mistakes, and
growing as you learn from those mistakes. While honoring traditional ideas about salvation, what if we are being judged not only
by what we do as individuals but also as members of communities, nations, and society? How do we, for example, treat our poor?
What has been our collective response to hate and intolerance?
Looking at a Christian mandate in this way puts more responsibility on us in the relationship with God to improve the quality of life
for all.

In one way, we spend our lives on earth in preparation for the
next thing, eternity. In another model, there is more urgency and
a greater focus on the now. The two ideas do not need to be mutu-
ally exclusive; however, by expanding into a sense of communal
salvation, we can find a greater sense of purpose in life. The mandate given is to love our neighbors—and the neighbor is everyone.
Forgiveness, mercy, and grace have been given to us by God. And,
in turn, we are inspired to show kindness and care to others. In our
journey, we have learned a little more about ourselves and about
who we are in relation to others. In this next chapter, we will bring
the love of God into the equation.

5. Volf, *Exclusion and Embrace*, 29.

3

Love Your God

IN CHAPTERS 1 AND 2, we discussed forming a deeper relationship with ourselves and with other people. In this chapter, I start with a discussion of evidence of the relational God in the Bible. Later, I outline the God of my own understanding and how I came to define God in this way. Being able to form an authentic relationship with God is a personal process that will take some time and some work. We often have to trust what we feel about God in our hearts, even when it is inconsistent with what others tell us about God. At the end of the chapter, I have added some questions for you to consider in a journal or in a small-group setting to help you define and hopefully connect with the God of your own understanding.

Relational God in the Bible

In the many examples of the relational God in the Bible, God appears to people, befriends them, and makes covenants with them. God intervenes to deliver military victories and provides relief to women who believe themselves to be barren. God provides water, food, and refuge to people in need. God shows favor to Moses, Abraham, Hagar, David, and Solomon. The New Testament is organized around the life and teachings of Jesus Christ, perhaps the best example of the relational God in the Bible.

I will always honor and respect faith traditions that believe that the Bible is the inerrant word of God. However, the tradition to which I belong allows for more flexibility and dynamic interaction with a living God. Although I believe that God is much more expansive than what is written in the Bible, I still study the Bible as an aspect of my spiritual practice. Over time, I have begun to consider Jesus, and not the Bible, as the Word of God.

The Gospel of John starts this way:

> In the beginning was the Word, and the Word was with God, and the Word was God. He was in the beginning with God. All things came into being through him, and without him not one thing came into being. What has come into being in him was life, and the life was the light of all people. The light shines in the darkness, and the darkness did not overcome it. (John 1:1–5)

By focusing on Jesus as the Word of God, the deepening and healing of the relationship between humankind and God can become the center of our faith. And we can focus on the message and meaning of Jesus, even when some of the details of the stories are hard to believe.

In Matthew 27:51, at the death of Jesus, the earth shakes, the rocks split, and the veil, or curtain, of the temple is split from top to bottom. In the Hebrew Scriptures, the curtain separated human beings from the holiest places in the temple, and only on certain occasions could the high priest enter the place where God dwells. When the curtain is torn, this represents the removal of all that separates us from God. We no longer need high priests or holy figures to act as intermediaries. We have direct access to God. Through the experience of Jesus, God experienced being human, and we were connected to the divine. In Romans 8:38–39, we learn that nothing can separate us from the love of God. Jesus is called Immanuel, which means "God with us." God is always with us. Through Jesus, the relationship between God and humanity becomes strengthened, and the cross and the torn curtain are symbols of that connection and the lengths to which God was willing to go to demonstrate God's love.

Considering Jesus as the Word of God, or God's Word, is our covenant with God. A covenant is stronger than a promise and deeper than friendship. The bond is unbreakable. Jesus offers himself as a path to connect with God and promises abundance in life. The testimony of the life and teachings of Jesus Christ is the strongest evidence of the relational God in the Bible. The relational God of the Bible loves all of humanity, and God's grace is extended to all, no matter the circumstances. There is nowhere outside of this divine grace. God is aligned with us in our personal struggles and with us when we suffer. Because of Jesus, we can have a direct, authentic connection with God, without an intermediary. And isn't that great news?

Relating to the God of Our Own Understanding

Like most people who grow up in church, I became a member of the unchurched as a young adult. I attended a large, African American Baptist church in my youth and participated in a worship service and gospel choir in college, but then became disenchanted with it all while I was in graduate school. My home church was a relatively progressive space for a Baptist church. However, as a young adult, my political views fell to the left of the rest of the community. I was a burgeoning feminist and radical lesbian. A space that once felt progressive on issues of racial justice felt conservative in its views on sexuality and gender. I did not stop believing in God, nor did I abandon my Christian faith, but I did begin to feel like the space of the church had become too stifling.

In my late twenties, I lived in Atlanta for a short time. People regularly approached me in the street and asked, "Do you have a church home?" I visited a couple of churches during that year and was shocked by the centrality of anti-gay rhetoric from the pulpit. I actually left one service when the preacher started to yell, "There is a plug and a socket, and that's how it has to be!" As much as I might have been critical of my home church, I remain grateful that I did not receive these kinds of hurtful and simplistic messages from the pulpit when I was young.

Like most adults who do find their way back to church, a tragedy in my life made me desire a return. At the time, I was grateful to my family for giving me such a solid foundation in Christianity and in the church. When I needed to go back, I was fortunate enough to live in a big city and have a sister in seminary. She helped me find a church where I could be black, gay, and Christian all at the same time. The Unity Fellowship Church in Brooklyn, New York, taught me that "God is love, and love is for everybody." They helped me to engage with the God of my own understanding. I encourage you to consider the ways that you understand God. Here, I will say a bit about my own.

Being part of a church as a child and belonging to a faithful and praying family were the foundation for my relationship with God. By the time I started a serious study of the Bible, I appreciated having a very strong foundation. Interestingly, I started to read the Bible simply because I became very tired of hearing, in response to bigotry, the phrase "It's in the Bible!" And I was not able to definitively argue whether it was or was not. In order to be able have some authority in my defense of social justice issues, I set my intentions on reading the Bible. With that narrow focus or reason in mind, I started Ted Cooper Jr.'s *Bible in Ninety Days Challenge*.[1] Reading the whole Bible in ninety days is as insane as it sounds. However, I never shy away from a challenge.

In my first attempt at reading the whole Bible, I did not read every word. However, through my efforts, I read more than I ever had before. My joy was finding bits and parts of the Bible that had worked their way into sermons, Christmas pageants, gospel songs, or American idioms. After this initial close reading of the Bible, I believed that I had the ammunition I would need to argue that there is no place in the Bible that says that God or Jesus hates gay people (or any group in particular). In no way is the focal point of the Bible the condemnation of LGBTQ+ people. In fact, there is very little in the Bible about sexuality at all. In order to base your theology on a message of intolerance for any group, you would

1. See Cooper, *Bible in 90 Days*.

have to ignore so much of the Bible, which emphasizes above all: love, mercy, and connectedness with God.

Even though I was feeling more confident, I participated in the challenge a second time. This time, I was better at keeping up with the pace. As I was reading the Bible the second time through, I had a kind of awakening. I felt like a light switch was turned on inside of me. I was on fire, and I wanted to learn more. I attended divinity school so I could learn from the experts and fill in the holes in my knowledge. As an adult student with no background in religion, I was surrounded by young people who knew more than I did about church history and theology. However, I believed that I could hold my own in knowledge of the biblical Scripture. At school, I was able to learn about how feminist, queer, and black liberation theologians interpreted the Bible and looked at social justice issues through a theological lens. I had engaged with theologians and began to find my own voice on issues of gender-based violence and discrimination against LGBTQ+ Christians by the church. My ideas about who God is come from reading the Bible through this new lens.

As I addressed above, it is challenging for progressive Christians to consider the Bible as the inerrant word of God. However, the way I see God has a lot to do with the overarching themes within both the Old and New Testaments. Embedded within the the Bible is the essence of who God is and some information about how God wants to be loved and worshipped. Running the risk of being too reductionist, the main theme of the Old Testament is that God wants us to put God first. Over and over again, people become distracted and are wayward, and God sends people and situations to compel them to get focused again. The literature of the New Testament focuses on the witness of Jesus Christ in the world. Jesus comes to fulfill promises made by God to save humanity in spite of itself and to fix a broken relationship between God and humankind. The messages of mercy, love, and compassion can be found as major themes throughout both sections of the Bible. If you pay attention to what is mentioned most often, the Bible teaches us that God is love.

Many people can read the same texts and have completely different ideas about what our goals should be as Christians. For example, those who argued against integration and interracial marriage in the first half of the twentieth century used the Bible for support. When I read the Bible, I hear support for nonviolent resistance of injustice of all kinds and for tolerance, love, and connection. Others hear something very different. What I do not believe is the idea that the Bible is a simple, straightforward, and clear guide for life. The Bible is a complex collection of texts, and what we read has been filtered through human interpretation. The Bible is useful but cannot be the only source for connecting with and relating to God.

One of the lessons that came out of my experience with the Unity Fellowship Church is that God cannot be limited to the pages of the Bible. There is no reason to believe that the Bible is the beginning and the end of all that God has to say to us. Ron Buford designed a slogan for The United Church of Christ that says "God is still speaking" and is symbolized by a comma. Buford was inspired by a quotation from Gracie Allen that says, "Never place a period where God has placed a comma."[2] The idea is that God is still active and engaged with humanity. What other literature, art, or music has been inspired by God? What can these things teach us?

I often find God speaking to me through literature. I read *The Shack* around the time when I became more serious about reading the Bible. William P. Young, author of *The Shack*, seems particularly inspired to me, and his reimagining of the Trinity was exciting. Being able to imagine that certain aspects of God are female and gender nonspecific resonated with me. I enjoyed the nontraditional image of God as a large, nurturing black woman and of Wisdom as a beautiful Latinx woman. *The Shack* also had very powerful messages about redemption, love, grief, and healing. I held on to a message that grace is extended to us all, because God can see the fullness of our experience and loves us unconditionally. God celebrates our "failures," because God sees that at the end of

2. "About the Comma," para. 1.

your attempts, you get it right! This very serious piece of fiction resonated with me in a deep way. Other fiction, like Alice Walker's *The Color Purple*, has helped me define relationality, as have key books on theology by Howard Thurman, Karen Baker-Fletcher, James Cone, and Delores Williams.

In addition to reading the Bible and other literature, my understanding of God has deepened through experience. God is always speaking to us. As I grow in my faith, I am learning how to hear God more clearly. When I was able to let go of a need to have a formal, articulate, and lengthy prayer in order for God to hear me, I was able to talk with God in the same way I would talk with any other person. I began to talk with God in the shower, on long walks, or in the car. For much of my life, I prayed only when things were bad and as a last resort. Now, I am able to talk with God about the things I want to see for my life and for the lives of the people I love. I can pray for additional compassion and to cope with everyday injustices. In addition to petitioning God, I also thank God over and over. Most prayers begin with "Thank you!" Words cannot express the gratitude I feel for all that I have, all that I have survived, and all the love that I have found during my journey. When openness in prayer is real, I can tap into deep emotions, and the tears begin to flow.

Talking with God feels natural and freeing. That said, I have to admit that *listening* can be a bit more challenging. The hard part is getting still enough to hear what God is saying to me. "Slow down!" is probably the message I receive most often these days. Listening to God involves trust. You have to trust God, and you have to trust that what you are hearing is God. When I am motivated by ego or fear, chances are the voice I am hearing is my own. Messages about expanding, forgiving others, and having the courage to love come from God. The voice of God I hear encourages movement and healing from past hurts as well as connection over isolation. The God of my understanding is all about mental health and clarity and hard truths. God's answers to my questions are sometimes "No!" and most often "Wait!"

At times, prayer is not about removing an obstacle but is about finding a way to cope while going through or around that obstacle. For many years, I suffered with chronic pain. Accepting that condition was very challenging, because I like to be in control. One night, the pain was so intense, I began to tremble and could not stop. I put my head on the pillow, pulled the covers over my head, and prayed. My prayer was simple. I said, "Please, help me!" I immediately began to feel something like a calm breeze pass over me. I was still shaking, but I was able to sleep. In the morning, the trembling had subsided. That night, I learned that, at times, God will not remove my afflictions; however, God will always be with me as I go through them.

As I begin to understand more about God, I am starting to believe that God already knows and understands me. God knows me. God can find me through songs on the radio. Messages sometimes come through other people, unbeknownst to them. Maybe some of the brilliant stuff I think I came up with in my conversations with others is actually a word from God. Sermons can often reach me in a deep way, and I often feel like these messages were written especially for me. With an open heart and open mind, I am able to have many receptors, and it has been interesting being able to understand what God is trying to tell me.

A passage in 1 Corinthians 12 says, "For now we see in a mirror, dimly, but then we will see face to face. Now I know only in part; then I will know fully, even as I have been fully known." I have found great comfort in the idea that I am fully known by God. Because of the nature of God, I do not have to try to be more than what I am. God understands what happened to my grandparents and my parents that led to the unique circumstances of my birth and my childhood. God has seen every mistake I have made and all of my wonderful strides towards self-improvement. Therefore, there is no need for me to be false or pretentious. I relish one relationship where I can be myself fully. Being accepted and loved unconditionally makes me want to do more and be a better person. I am not looking for favor or rewards; I am motivated by gratitude. The love I receive also makes me want to love others in return. I want to forgive and be generous, because that's the way I am being treated. I am nowhere near being patient enough, but I am working on it. I celebrate that God, who is in touch with who I am and knows all that I will become, loves me unconditionally.

One of the most important lessons I've learned over the years is to trust God. In the past, the thing about which I have worried the most is money. More specifically, I worried about not having enough money. Being preoccupied with making ends meet and the consequences of late or unpaid bills was a major part of my childhood. These worries increased as I became responsible for my own bills and had dreams I wanted to fulfill. No aspect of my life has been a smooth road. Rather, my path has felt more like an old, rickety roller coaster rife with uncertainty and crazy ups and downs. Each time things would get bad financially, I spent a great deal of time worrying. And, then, as a last resort, I would pray.

Once, I wrote down all my worries on a sheet of paper and folded it into the pages of my Bible. A few years later, I was looking for something in my Bible, and the list fell out. I had to laugh at myself, because it took me a minute to remember what the note was about. All of the items on my list had been addressed so thoroughly that I had forgotten about the list altogether. Apparently, God had not forgotten about my list and my needs. What I realized as well was that many of my problems were solved when I asked for help from other people. Many of the solutions did not involve money at all. As I am writing this, there has been no major financial breakthrough, but I have learned that being worried about money or anything is a choice. I am getting better at remembering to ask other people for help.

God has the full picture. I cannot see everything clearly now, and so I trust God. Not worrying can sometimes feel like a full-time effort. Because I have spent so much of my life feeling anxious and worried, I find it difficult not to fall back into familiar patterns when problems arise. That said, I am beginning to believe that trusting God means trusting God fully. Because of my relationship with God, I feel better equipped to handle the storms of life. Instead of saying "Everything will be all right," I now say, "I will be all right within everything." This attitude is very empowering. The more I open my heart to God, the deeper our relationship becomes. I have a healthy, solid, lasting, and real relationship with God, which I work on every day.

In forming a relationship with the God of one's understanding, there will be many things we will never understand. Theodicy is a unique branch of theological inquiry that asks, "How is it that we can believe God is good when there is so much evil in the world?" Theodicy means "justifying God," and German philosopher Gottfried Wilhelm Leibniz coined the term in his book of the same title.[3] Theologians address this question in different ways. Some theologians argue that God is able to do all things and chooses not to intervene; and others believe that God is not able to intervene in all things. The latter group believes that there is evil that operates outside of God's control. These are questions with which you may want to wrestle for yourself. These are important questions to consider, especially as you cope with hardship in life, including injustice, suffering, grief, and loss. I also imagine it would be difficult to form a relationship with God if you believe God causes you harm or watches idly as you suffer.

I tend to believe that God can do anything but for reasons outside of my understanding chooses what to do and what not to do. I do not know why God does not intervene at all times; however, I am starting to believe that it has a lot to do with our responsibility as collaborators in making life better for everyone. In a different project, I am exploring the theme of theodicy within African American or black liberation theology. Even as enslaved people experienced terror, humiliation, and abuse, they formed an enduring and unique Christian faith tailored to coping with racism in America. There is a tradition of creating a "canon within a canon" to resist biblical texts that were used to support obedience and subjugation.[4] The space of the black church allowed people who felt invisible and overlooked by society to be built up through

3. Leibniz, *Theodicy*.

4. Williams, *Sisters in the Wilderness*, and Brown Douglas, *Sexuality and the Black Church*.

spirituals and sermons and by holding positions of leadership in the church.

Theodicy is a theme within the work of black liberation theologians. What I found is that African Americans have formed a very pragmatic understanding of life with its ups and downs. In spite of hard times, God is with us and for us. A number of theologians have associated Jesus's experience on the cross with the humiliating and painful death of a victim of lynching. The cross becomes a symbol that God is aligned with African Americans in their suffering, in lynching and in other forms of unwarranted violence due to racism. Most importantly, the resurrection symbolizes victory over death and over all suffering that happens in life. In our current moment, many church communities are finding ways to eradicate structural racism and to help through education and economic and spiritual reparations. To the extent that some suffering, like in the case of racism, is being caused by human behavior, we have a responsibility to do the work of social change. There are times when God does not intervene because the work that needs to be done is our own.

The most important lessons I've learned on my journey are that there is no prerequisite for gaining access to God's love and that there is no place outside of God's grace. At the end of each service at the church I attended as a child, the choir would line up in the hall and sing a portion of Jude 1:24 into the sanctuary. They would sing, "Now unto him that is able to keep you from falling." We can no longer fall from grace. The need for separation between God and humankind, and between all of us, ended with the death of Jesus. The work that is left to do is to bring people who have been pushed to the margins back into the fold and to convince those with abundance to share. I believe in a Christianity that focuses on faith and love and running towards God's open embrace, rather than one about narrowly escaping hell. God rewards love with love. The impetus to do better and to live a better life comes from a place of wholeness and appreciation.

My final thoughts about the God of my understanding are about God and change. Many faith traditions teach that God never changes. I understand this sentiment, because in a life where things are unpredictable, it is comforting to know that God will stay the same. But, I have often wondered why we believe God would not change. If you believe that God is the author and creator of all things related to nature (for example), it seems that everything in nature is constantly changing. As the seasons change, the leaves on the trees change color and then fall off. In the spring, the flowers bloom on the branches and then the leaves return. Then the cycle begins again. We all change. We have an accelerated change in the beginning as our bodies and brains develop. Then, we grow. We learn and apply new lessons to our lives. Our bodies are constantly changing. Everything is constantly changing, bit by bit and sometimes in ways we cannot perceive. Why, then, do we believe that God would not change? Perhaps, it is comforting to believe in a God that never changes because of our own discomfort around change. Change is associated with bad circumstances. I am starting to see change as neither good nor bad. Change simply is. My attitude about the change is what makes me apply one label or another to that situation.

I wanted to share a bit about the God of my own understanding and how I came to that understanding in hopes that you might also begin to consider the ways in which you understand God. Religion is often presented to us in a sharp dichotomy: you either believe everything without question, or you must walk away from religion completely. At its best, religion is a way to connect with, and to understand, something beyond our understanding. As I discussed early, relational theology and other forms of liberation theology allow for some flexibility and creative exploration in forming that connection. We have permission to discern and to ask God questions directly.

Where Do You Find God?

Prayer and meditation are the best ways to open up communication with God. Prayer allows you to ask, and meditation (or stillness) opens you up to hear answers. Prayer does not have to be sophisticated or even formal. You do not have to search for the right words to say. Talk with God directly, and petition God for yourself and on behalf of others. I talk with God a lot; however, there are times when I connect with God in a more formal way. I always start with gratitude. Next, I ask God for the things I need. Mostly, I ask for more compassion in situations where people are difficult to love. I have also begun to ask God to help me have a better attitude about my adversity rather than an escape from it. From childhood, I end my prayers by blessing people. I start with the people who are in the forefront of my mind. Some are there for all the wrong reasons. Meditation opens up your receptors. The more you open up, the more spaces there will be to hear God and to see God reflected in the faces and behaviors of others. Finally, remember, there is no such thing as being outside of God's grace. The open arms of Jesus represent a welcome that never expires. It doesn't matter how long you are away; God is here enthusiastically awaiting your return to love.

The following are some questions you can answer in a journal or in small-group discussions to identify the contours of the God of your understanding. However, first I want to list a set of assumptions:

1. You are loved by God. You are lovable, worthwhile, and one who is an important part of the whole.

2. God is all that is love. If something is not love, that something is not God.

3. You can trust God.

4. God sees you and loves and accepts you, just as you are.

5. God cares about you.

Questions:

• What does being a Christian mean to you? How has your idea about that identity changed over time?

- In what ways can this concept of Jesus as the Word of God (as a promise that was fulfilled) help to shape your connection with God?

- John 14:27 explains that Jesus gives us a sense of peace that the world cannot take away. How do you define peace?

- When did you feel the most at peace in your life? What aspects of those moments can you incorporate into your daily life?

- How do you feel about the mystery (about all the nature of God that we will never know)? Does the uncertainty make you uncomfortable?

- What external messages about God resonate with what you feel in your heart? And what messages are inconsistent?

As a culture, we seem invested in promoting a wrath-filled and hateful God. However, when we can be honest with ourselves, we recognize that the God at work in our lives is actually tender and loving. The experience or the lesson may be very difficult, but God is the joy within it. God is in the birth of a child, the forgiveness of someone who has hurt you in a deep way, and in the grief of lost loves. God is comfort when you are feeling abandoned, abused, betrayed, alone, or scared. God is the love you feel when you hear the sound of your loved one's voice or a beautiful gospel song. God is the joy you feel when you see a rainbow and the awesome feeling of smallness as you stand on the beach.

Not everything works out the way you want it to. Life is hard. When you can, release the idea that God is punishing you or that you have done something so bad that God cannot possibly love you. When you can, let go of the belief that the only reason to do good things is to get rewards—here or in an afterlife. When you can do so, life will make more sense. You will live with a greater sense of purpose. You will have confidence in your ability to handle whatever comes along, and you'll know you don't have to go through it alone. You will find more and more moments of peace.

Relational theology has guided our journey together where we examined self-love and self-care, discussed extending that care to others, and then reframed that powerful energy as expressions of love for God. I talked about my own experiences, both the brokenness of past hurts and the path towards a closer relationship with God. I used my own experience, as well as theory from relational and liberation theologies, to demonstrate the connections between self, other, and God that is outlined in Matthew 27:37–39. People who identify as Christian but cannot find what they need in the context of a church, as well as those who have been driven away or turned off by the experience of going to church, should not feel like they have to forgo a relationship with God. The process of forming a real relationship with a living God has an exciting way of bringing you into connection and community with others and gives your life greater purpose. Relational theology invites us to have greater responsibility for creating an abundant life for ourselves and for others and asks us to value interdependence. Once your connection with God is close, you become bolder in your strivings for social justice and less fearful in the face of your own challenges.

Chapter 4 is written specifically for people who have left church as the result of clergy sexual abuse or other abuse in the context of religion or the church. The appendices provide more tools for your exploration into deeper relationship with God.

4

If You Experienced Abuse at
Church . . .

I wanted to devote a chapter to you if you left church because
of child sexual abuse at the hands of clergy, or due to spiritual or
ritual abuse in the context of religion. We will never know how
many people have become unchurched because of a trauma that
happened in church or at the hands of a religious leader. I would
argue that most people who have broken ties with the church or
organized religion fit into one of these three categories. If you take
away only one message from this chapter, please understand that
you are not alone.

Abuse at Church

Clergy child sexual abuse (CSA), ritual abuse, and spiritual abuse
are three experiences that might drive a person out of church
and organized religion altogether. I start this section by providing definitions for each of these terms, because giving language
to our pain can often be an important step in the healing process.
When child predators and perpetrators of crime are caught, we
tend to focus on criminal justice and civil litigation. We spend
less time focused on survivors and how their trauma is having an
impact on their spiritual lives. Faith is often where you turn in the

process of healing. To be damaged spiritually is a tragedy in and of itself. My worry is that, as people who were hurt in the context of religion leave the church, they also walk away from a relationship with God. If you have been hurt in this way, the trust and connection integral to forming (or repairing) a relationship with God and with God's people will be more difficult to attain. In spite of the challenges, there is still hope. In time, you will begin to see God as separate from a person (or people) who caused you harm in the name of God. Throughout this process, be as gracious and generous as you can with yourself as you heal.

In the latter part of the twentieth century, scandals in the Catholic Church made us more aware of CSA that happens at the hands of clergy or other religious or lay leaders in the church. The Rape Abuse Incest National Network (RAINN) website offers this definition of CSA:

> Child sexual abuse is a form of child abuse that includes sexual activity with a minor. A child cannot consent to any form of sexual activity, period. When a perpetrator engages with a child this way, they are committing a crime that can have lasting effects on the victim for years. Child sexual abuse does not need to include physical contact between a perpetrator and a child.

People who sexually abuse children have a similar pattern of finding ways to be around a lot of children, grooming their victims, desensitizing the victim to inappropriate behavior, and threatening a child to maintain secrecy. What is important to understand is that clergy who sexually abuse children have the same behavior and motives as predators who are not clergy. In a very important article, researchers Dale and Alpert compared the information we have about child predators and found similar patterns and tactics used by priests who abuse.[1] The article emphasizes that clergy CSA is not a new phenomenon. In the past, the power structure within the Catholic Church responded to the issue in a way that often favored protecting the priest and the reputation of the Catholic

---

1. Dale and Alpert, "Hiding behind the Cloth."

Church over the protection of children. Priests who were known to be sexual predators were removed and sent to other parishes. A few received various forms of "treatment"; however, they were moved into communities that did not receive any warning. And most continued their behavior. In some instances, families of victims were threatened and silenced. And like many incidents of CSA, much of the abuse went unreported.

As brave victims and their families worked to fight against cover-ups and demand that people in positions of power be held accountable, society tried to understand why there was seemingly so much abuse in this population. Some believed that the vow of celibacy turned priests into sexual predators. There was also an effort to conflate the sexual abuse of boys by men with homo-sexuality. Others placed the responsibility on the institution of the Catholic Church, which allowed the abuse to go on unchecked. What Dale and Alpert posit, and I find credible, is that some child predators *become* priests in order to have unfettered access to children and the trust of families and communities. These are not men who are called by God to serve communities of faith. These are people who hide behind their profession to do what they want to do, which is to harm children. Like Boy Scouts and other youth organizations, schools, sports teams, and other youth activities, churches have been a space where the right person can gain the trust of the community and have free reign to damage lives.

As adults, people who were victimized as children always look back and ask: Was there something about me that made me chosen as a victim? Did I do something to encourage it? Why didn't I stop it? And why didn't I tell anyone? Child predators are focused and intentional. On average, before a child predator is caught, they have abused dozens of other victims. They practice and get more effective at recruiting victims and hiding their behavior from others. Clergy predators prey on innocence and manipulate children, parents, institutions, and their communities.

When you are chosen to be a victim, a predator is looking for two things: access and opportunity. They want to create a situation where they can get away with what they are doing for as long as possible. They do not want you to tell or get help, and they do not want to get caught. Grooming is the process predators use to get close to their victim. Clergy abusers are in a position to groom both the child and their parents. You would trust your priest to take your child on a trip. You would trust that the counselors in youth Bible study or church summer camp to keep your child safe. In an environment as open as the church once was, clergy abusers could do a lot of damage.

Predators also work very hard to get their victim to stay silent, and this can be in the form of threats or through manipulation. They can tell that child that she is to blame for her own abuse. The most insidious aspect of clergy CSA is that a clergyperson can tell a child that God wants her to do whatever the clergyperson says to do. A child might be threatened with hell or eternal damnation for her family. Family and society both reinforce a message of obedience to clergypersons, making reporting an incident that much more complicated. The level of authority of a priest gives them the highest level of responsibility for being respectful and careful in their interactions with people. Outside of incest (the abuse of children by their own parents), clergy CSA is the most complicated to untangle emotionally. Church is supposed to be a place where children can feel safe. A child enters into a relationship with an adult needing help, spiritual guidance, extra attention, or love, and in return is exploited and used for the clergyperson's own sexual needs. Clergy CSA is truly heartbreaking.

Ritual abuse may also involve a clergy person or lay leader, but the abuse is part of a system and is infused into a person's home and church life. First Person Plural, a dissociative identity disorders organization in the United Kingdom, defines ritual abuse as:

> A complex mix of sexual, physical, psychological, emotional and spiritual abuse . . . which often begins in infancy or early childhood. The abuse is premediated, systematic and sustained over a long period of time. All the abuse is justified by the perpetrators with reference to a faith or belief system and, in the group setting, is

performed as an integral part of that belief system's rituals.[2]

Ritual abuse requires both a doctrine that can be religious (or couched in religious ideology) and a very strict, authoritarian culture.

For the people inside the culture, the world is divided into those who belong and outsiders. Those who maintain power do so through emotional and psychological manipulation, violence, and torture. Leaders enlist participants to monitor and punish each other to keep everyone in line. Because the community is so insulated, the idea of reaching out to someone outside the community for help will most likely not seem like an option. Ritual abuse often includes mind control, sexual abuse, and very extreme forms of physical abuse.[3] The abuse is used to indoctrinate people into the belief system.

Like ritual abuse, spiritual abuse occurs most often in religious cultures that are strict and authoritarian. Spiritual abuse occurs when a clergyperson or lay leader inflicts "abuse on congregation members, often by creating a toxic culture within the church or group by shaming or controlling members using the power of their position."[4] Leaders can use that control to gain obedience, money, or sexual favors. Public humiliation and shame are tools used by perpetrators to control what women in the church wear and to terrorize teens questioning their sexuality.

Spiritual abuse often happens in charismatic and evangelical worship spaces, although not exclusively. The abuse is part of a system where hierarchy and obedience are required for participation.[5] Worship spaces are organized around one charismatic yet self-serving leader. As more information surfaces about spiritual abuse, survivors benefit from being able to name what

2. "Definition of Ritual Abuse," para. 6.

2. Scott, *Politics and Experience.*

3. "What Is Spiritual Abuse?," para. 1.

4. Johnson and VanVonderen, *Subtle Power.*

they have experienced. Survivors of spiritual abuse have deep spiritual wounds and are working through shame, isolation, and self-loathing.[6]

One form of spiritual abuse which is very common happens when Scripture is used to promote the abuse or the expulsion of LGBTQ+ people from the church. People who identify as LGBTQ+ or those who are perceived to be gay are degraded, humiliated, and harassed regularly in church spaces. For African Americans and other Christians of color, the church is a safe haven from the daily assault of living in a racist society. To be rejected by one's church in this setting, I argue, is akin to human rights abuse. Of course, the black church is not the only space where intolerance towards LGBTQ+ persons comes from the pulpit. Bigotry causes a great deal of pain and self-loathing in victims.

Anti-gay attitudes that are fostered by the church can seep into the home life and into the community. Bigots harass and assault LGBTQ+ people, and parents drive their LGBTQ+ children into homelessness, because they believe the Bible supports their actions. I have added a section in the appendix with a short discussion about the Scripture that has been used to promote homophobia. I also list some books that delve deeper into the issue of LGBTQ+ inclusion in the body of Christ. There simply is so much more evidence in the Bible that God is love than there is that God has disdain towards LGBTQ+ persons. Therefore, we should focus on God's love. I never want to be disrespectful of people who believe that the Bible is the inerrant word of God and interpret various passages in the Bible with a firm belief that homosexuality is sin. And I understand that many of us have a different perspective on the interpretation and the *meaning* of Scripture. Regardless of a difference of opinion, spiritual abuse is never okay. No one should be forced to choose between being "in the closet" at church or being abused for being out.

6. Oakley and Kinmond, *Breaking the Silence*.

If You Experienced Abuse in the Church, You Are Not Alone!

I am talking about clergy CSA, spiritual abuse, and ritual abuse, because more than anything, these are probably the main reasons people leave church for good. Church should be a place of comfort, peace, connection, and inspiration. A worship experience should never make you feel like you are unsafe.

As discussed earlier, I am a survivor of CSA, although I did not experience my abuse at the hands of clergy or in a church setting. The hardest parts for me to overcome have been the isolation and the silence. I have a very difficult time connecting with and trusting people, and life's many disappointments have left me unable to trust myself when opening up to new people. Whether you are told not to tell others or not, the message becomes very clear and is reinforced through the silence and your own feelings of shame. More than forty years later, I still believe that I am causing harm to others when I talk about my abuse. And I do not want to shame or embarrass my family. Being victimized in childhood makes the simple, good things in life a bit more challenging. I can only imagine how much more difficult a climb it would be for someone hurt within the context of religion. All of us who are part of a congregation put our trust into its leaders to keep us safe from harm. We are doing what we believe is right in order to save our souls. The damage done by the betrayal of trust is tremendous.

If you experienced clergy CSA, ritual abuse, or spiritual abuse, then your path to connection (or reconnection) is going to be very difficult. You were harmed in ways that will make trust and connection challenging. Have compassion for yourself in the process, and take your time. In listening to survivors of CSA and sexual assault, inside and outside of church settings, I have heard many express anger with God. People have said to me that "God watched what was happening and did nothing," "God caused it to happen because I was bad," and "God enjoyed watching me suffer." How much harder must it be to let go of these messages, if the person doing the harm is a member of the clergy or is the one feeding you the message in the first place? At our core, we all struggle with the question about why a God who is with us and for us would also allow our suffering at the hands of others. And I do not have an answer to that. I find comfort in a belief that God is embedded in the process between harm and healing. God brings into our lives that someone who treats us with compassion in the midst of hard challenges. And God is the inspiration and source of courage for those people who dedicate their lives to changing laws, policies, and public perception around abuse, in order to save the lives of others.

As you begin your healing journey, start by telling your story. Telling your story breaks the isolation and silence in your own experience and inspires others to share as well. Abusers take the time to groom their victims and put a lot of energy into isolating them from other people. Their central motivation is to keep the abuse going as long as possible. They need to keep you from telling other people, so they will not get in trouble or have to stop what they are doing. Long after the abuse ends, the isolation and the fear of telling others can stay with you. If you have the support you need, you may decide somewhere in your process to seek a legal remedy. And, if you never go through the courts, that is fine, too. At the beginning of the process, the goal is your own healing. All that said, you need to tell someone. If you do not have someone you can trust enough to tell, tell yourself. Write it down in a journal or in a letter you never send to your abuser. If you live with others who may come across what you wrote, burn or rip up what you have written after you get it all out. The process of telling, even just yourself, takes your power back. You will take your voice back from someone who wanted to silence you permanently.

"Clergy CSA," "ritual abuse," and "spiritual abuse" are terms that may help survivors in the healing process. Sometimes, it is good to be able to put language to something you have experienced. The effort to name violence against women and children has picked up steam only in the last fifty or sixty years. Labels like "domestic violence," "date or acquaintance rape," and "stalking," for example, have helped society and law enforcement become aware of these issues. If you were a victim of violence before there was widely acknowledged language around it, it may have been harder to understand that what happened was really wrong. A number of advocacy organizations were founded by people who were once victims. There are more resources now than ever before. Being able to name what happened brings you into community with others who understand how you feel. You learn that what happened to you was not your fault. The brave men and women who first stepped up to talk about clergy abuse in the Catholic Church were survivors and their families. Their perseverance has made a major impact on society. It is now much more difficult to get away with such behavior. There are more of us watching out for children. We have developed the language and tools to fight against this form of abuse.

Minimizing is a coping strategy used by victims of child abuse. One might say, "Oh, it wasn't that bad" or "Well, I turned out okay, so it doesn't matter." Within Christian settings, we can sometimes minimize our own hardship by comparing what we went through to Jesus's experience on the cross. Some Christians believe that the only way to redemption is through suffering alongside Jesus on the cross, and others compare their own pain to that of Jesus and use that to minimize what happened. Jesus suffered and died on the cross for us. Making the ultimate sacrifice was his task alone. The point of Jesus's suffering on the cross is that God is aligned with us in the ways that we suffer as humankind. Jesus's resurrection on Easter represents God's victory over death, as well as the pain and suffering we go through in life. So, we do not have to minimize or downplay our pain for ourselves or for others. Instead, we can be reassured that God will walk with us along our healing process.

As a faith leader, I find it particularly painful to learn about other leaders using their power for their own gratification. People who are called to serve God are servant leaders. We are in it for the people we serve and to promote the will of God. People who are in it for themselves have joined our profession for the wrong reasons. Under no circumstance is what happened to you appropriate. In the second wave of the feminist movement in the U.S., women adopted the phrase "the personal is political." Mostly focused on the issues of domestic violence, the slogan told women that they were not alone in their experience of abuse. And that the tolerance of violence against women was a broader societal concern. Sexism in society helped to perpetuate a woman's experience in the home. Similarly, systems like that of the Catholic Church or other institutions where abuse occured, like schools or youth organizations, perpetuated violence through cover-ups and pressure. There is room for all of us, victims or not, to advocate for institutions and leaders to be held accountable for crimes in the past. No matter how long ago the damage happened, victims still need to find their way to justice. Clergy should be in the forefront of creating pressure on churches to have those who work with children get background checks and to take all available precautions to keep children safe. We need to make people aware of the damage this kind of behavior can cause to children, families, and congregations as a whole.

If You Experienced Abuse in Church, There Is Hope in the Healing!

When you have experienced clergy CSA, ritual abuse, or spiritual abuse, hope can be a dangerous thing. I imagine that some of the ways we talk about God as father or parent can be challenging for you if you have been abused. God is an all-powerful entity; even if the entity is kind, there is something disturbing about being watched or something that feels transactional about receiving protection. We can sometimes consider a relationship with Jesus as a friend, and perhaps seeing God this way can be helpful as well. The safest place to start may be connecting with the God within. There, seeing the face of God happens when you look in the mirror. The important thing to consider is that God is entirely different from the God that was presented to you in the context of abuse.

I am a believer that things that are broken in the context of relationship can be mended through connection. If you are not quite ready to talk about your past with other people, you can start by reading books on the topic and access resources on websites until you are ready. Get help through therapy as an individual or in a group by joining or starting a support group. Mostly, be patient with yourself in this process. My hope is that you are able to find God on your path to healing.

My go-to resources for CSA are RAINN and 1in6 (a resource specifically for male survivors).[7] I also have found a website helpful for learning more about survivors of clergy abuse[8] and a website for women survivors of all forms of abuse, including clergy abuse.[9] *The Dinah Project* is a resource guide for clergy who would like to talk about the issue of sexual abuse and assault.[10] *The Courage to Heal* is a classic workbook for survivors that was written in the 1980s and is still helpful and relevant today.[11] The authors produced additional workbooks for caregivers and loved ones, and one of them produced a book with testimony called *I Never Told Anyone*,[12] a book I found very helpful in my own process. Finally, *Outgrowing the Pain: A Book for and about Adults Abused as Children*[13] is one I would recommend to anyone dealing with this pain for the first time. It is a short book, with illustrations, to which I find myself returning time and again.

Remember, the abuse that happened to you is not your fault.

Remember, you are not alone!

Remember, whatever you did/do to survive is okay.

Remember, in time, you will have the victory over your pain.

7. www.rainn.org; 1in6.org.

8. www.snapnetwork.org.

9. www.takingbackourselves.org.

10. Coleman, *Dinah Project*.

11. Bass and Davis, *Courage to Heal*.

12. Bass and Thornton, *I Never Told Anyone*.

13. Gil, *Outgrowing the Pain*.

Appendix A

To Church or Not to Church? . . .
That Is the Question!

UNDER THE RIGHT CIRCUMSTANCES, attending church can be a great way to connect with other like-minded people. Even though my goal in writing this book is not to get you into church, you may decide to look for a church one day. In this section, I will say a few words about how to choose a church, should you want to connect with God in that way. With the right fit, you will be able to find a space where you can be spiritually fed on a regular basis. You may even be able to express your gifts and become involved in the social justice work done by the church. Here are some things you should consider when trying to find a new church community.

Ideally, a church would:

- help you learn more about the nature of God
- introduce you to the Bible (while also providing opportunities for you to agree or not with the interpretation of text)
- connect you with the community inside the church, a local community (through service) outside the church, and a broader Christian community

That said, if you do choose to go to church, think about finding a church community that is similar to your values and meets your needs. Instead of trying to fit into the model of the church, search until you find something that works for you.

Here, I have divided churches into three categories: low-relational, medium-relational, and high-relational, based on the likelihood that one can develop a relationship with God in that institution.

Low-Relational Church

In a low-relational church—you may be harmed physically, mentally, or spiritually. Your money may be stolen. Abuse (either verbal, physical, or sexual) is tolerated. The central message is hatred or the fear of others. You are encouraged to treat people who do not believe what you believe poorly. Children are encouraged to hate and to bully other people. Fear is used for motivation. You may be shamed or prevented from taking Communion if you acted "sinfully" the night before. Rejection of LGBTQ+ people is believed to be God's mandate. The congregation is too small (one family and you) or too large or loud, making you feel like you are in a rock concert. Although the church calls itself "Bible-based," there is only one very limited interpretation being tolerated. Segregation, homophobia, and xenophobia are presented as necessary. Worship is organized around one megalomaniac. Anything besides God, Jesus, or love is being worshipped—money, maleness, the pastor, etc.

In the low-relational church, the figurative concept of "the enemy" that is mentioned in the Bible is assigned to groups of people—like Muslims, Jewish people, or people of color—and then parts of the Bible that mention "destroying the enemy" become applied in a dangerous way. If any of these things are present in a church, there is a low possibility of developing any sort of relationship with God as a result of attending church.

Medium-Relational Church

In a medium-relational church—you are welcomed. All strangers are incorporated into the community in a loving/nonconfrontational way. The central message from the pulpit is about love, God, and Jesus. You are asked to focus on God and guided through the Bible. You are encouraged to give your time, talent, and/or treasures—and you are thanked, even when you don't have anything to give. Belonging to this church makes you feel good, renewed. You feel like part of a broader community of people who are not perfect but are working to further good in the world.

High-Relational Church

The high-relational church—has the same qualities as the medium-relational church, but they are more explicit about their effort to be inclusive of everyone. This church recognizes that they will have to make even more of an effort to demonstrate the inclusion and affirmation of LGBTQ+ people and their families (by flying a rainbow flag). If they realize that the congregation is cis-gender or segregated, they will make the effort to provide Anti-Racism and Trans 101 education for the leadership and the congregation, to create diversity. The church leadership actively works to dismantle systems of oppression and are vocal and visible social change agents. This church provides opportunities for members of the congregation to feed the hungry and give comfort to the afflicted.

Further, high-relational churches are open, flexible, and change often. They incorporate opportunities for interfaith connection and exchange. These churches promote respect for other faith practices and religions. And, they provide community-based opportunities to fellowship with the unchurched. At the center of this church is the experience of finding a healthy and loving relationship with God.

No one should ever feel abused or fearful in the context of a church. Church should be a space where people can connect with others and receive the support and encouragement they need, both physically and spiritually. Churches at their best provide many different opportunities for people to plug into service work and to engage in social issues.

Appendix B

Three Five-Minute Bible Study Lessons

As we discussed earlier, the Bible does not tell the complete story of who God is; however, there are many examples of a relational God and power in relation in the Bible. In this final section of this book, I want to let you know that there is more than one way to interpret the Bible and more liberal ways of understanding Christianity. Conservative Christianity tends to get more airplay in our culture. Rigid interpretations and a literal reading of the Bible make Christianity seem illogical. The Bible is too complex to be considered a straightforward guide for life. The Bible is not a straightforward document. You have to work very hard to gather meaning from the Bible. Also, the Bible is not one document. It is better to think of the Bible as a collection of diverse documents—written at various times, by different people, with different agendas. The documents were written in many languages, and throughout time, people made choices about which books would be included in the canon and which would not. Choices needed to be made about how to update certain words from ancient languages into modern conversational English. Scholars struggle and theologians debate about the meanings, but it is rare that any of this information trickles down to those of us reading the text on a regular basis. I am hoping that relational theology can provide for some necessary "wiggle room" in the way that you relate to the Bible and to your Christian faith.

Many of us were raised in traditions where we were told that the Bible was written by God—if not by God's hand, then by devout humans channeling what God told them to write. Under the best of circumstances, we can believe that the writers of Scripture were inspired by God. When we are trying to understand the nature of God, we have to keep in mind that the writers were limited by a human understanding of that which cannot be understood by humans. Hopefully, they were devout and did their best. However, because they were human, they were limited by their social context. Because they were all most likely male, they were limited by their cultural understanding of the place of women and how women should behave. They even fashioned whole stories where women do not appear at all. My favorite stories are the ones in which men sit down to eat. Are we supposed to believe that they cooked a meal for themselves? What is missing from the stories are the women who prepare the meals, clean the homes, and raise the boys who become the great men of the Bible. This is just one example of ways that we can fill in the gaps within stories to find deeper meaning in what we read.

Within feminist theology, there is a concept called the hermeneutics of suspicion. "The strategy is to interpret a biblical text and its Christian receptions, mindful that both have been largely shaped by male perspectives without attention to those of women."[1] Reading biblical texts with suspicion allows us to ask questions like "Where are all the women when this event is taking place?" Then, reading the Bible becomes a creative process that helps us all feel connected to the text. Reading with suspicion also reinforces the idea that texts are influenced by the cultural context of the author and of the intended audience.

It is important to read knowing that a host of things may be at work (some of which have nothing to do with religion or God) within the Bible. I struggle with a lot of things I read in the Bible.

---

1. Clifford, "Feminist Hermeneutics." See also Schüssler Fiorenza, *Bread Not Stone.*

Many people in the communities I serve would like to throw the book out. For me, there is a certain beauty in a lot of Scripture. I like reading something that connects me to something my ancestors read and cherished. I also value the complexities and enjoy grappling with different concepts. Struggling with the parts that are inconsistent with the way we see God is important and is part of growing in faith.

For our purposes here, we will examine three texts—one from the Old Testament, one from the Gospels, and one from the Epistles. I have provided a short synopsis and three questions to consider. Finally, I have provided some brief notes about the discussion of homosexuality in the Bible.

Three Five-Minute Bible Study Lessons

Lesson One: Psalm 23
"The Lord is my shepherd, I shall not want."

In trying to consider three must-read texts from the Bible, the Twenty-Third Psalm would be on the top of my list. Many people commit this psalm to memory, and I recommend you do (if you have not already). This psalm has beautiful imagery and a message of comfort that you may find helpful when things get tough. Because I grew up in an urban context, I found it helpful to learn that the agrarian-focused concepts in the Bible were crafted for an audience of people closer to the land. A shepherd would evoke strong feelings of a person who was a provider and a protector. The Twenty-Third Psalm is timeless, because even being outside of this context, we can understand a shepherd as someone we would trust and someone we would follow.

As we follow the shepherd, they take us to a place that is peaceful—a place of green pastures and still waters. They lead us to a place where our soul can be restored. Because of this protection, we do not have to be afraid. Additionally, we may find ourselves at a table "in the presence of our enemies." This is when we are abandoned or betrayed by those we have come to trust. These are the times when we are at the decision-making table, working to speak for those who are not represented. The psalmist says that at the table God anoints your head with oil. God is with us! Our heads are anointed, because God's love and protection puts us in a positive headspace. "My cup overflows." The abundance in life is ours. The line that says "Surely goodness and mercy shall follow me all the days of my life," is very comforting. Things are not always going to go our way; however, knowing that God is with us can bring additional comfort.

Read also Psalm 121, and listen to Bobby McFerrin's "The 23rd Psalm (dedicated to my mother)."

Questions:

(1) Consider the analogy in Psalm 23 of sitting at a table with my enemies. What about that imagery resonates with you?

(2) Psalm 23 also has lovely images evoking peace and calm. What spaces in nature have served as a refuge for you?

(3) What do you feel has been the appeal of the Twenty-Third Psalm through the ages?

Lesson Two: Romans 8:28–39
"Who will separate us from the love of Christ?"

The letters in the Bible that are attributed to Paul come under scrutiny, because they are often used to justify homophobia and the exclusion of women from the pulpit. It helps me to think of Paul as a religious zealot; he was an outsider advocating for his own right to belong. In spite of the problematic moments in the letters, there are some very beautiful concepts defining love and God's love for us through Christ. Romans 8 has moved me to tears many times. If you can, read the whole chapter. There are so many great things to unpack about being adopted as brothers, sisters, and siblings in Christ. The imagery of labor pains and the anticipation of a new world to come. And the idea of a choice, which is demonstrated by imagery of fear, darkness, and bondage juxtaposed with light, hope, and freedom.

Romans 8:28 says, "We know that all things work together for those who love God, who are called according to his purpose." Similar to the hope in the words "surely goodness and mercy shall follow me all the days of my life," from Psalm 23, this line feels hopeful and comforting. And, we all know that very often things do not work out as we plan, and "bad things" continue to happen to "good people"; however, this has always made me think that there is a bigger picture to which I am not privy. We can trust that God is on our side and will help us find a way to make even the worst experiences into the good for the whole.

Romans 8:31b asks, "If God is for us, who is against us?" And, Romans 8:34 asks, "Who is to condemn?" The followers of Christ have always been countercultural. As Christians in America, we may not currently face the persecution described by Paul; however, those who work against materialism, inequality, or segregation face hard challenges. Our work takes courage. Loving and forgiving others takes courage. In Romans 8:37, we are referred to as "more than conquerors!" We can feel encouraged as the bold followers of Christ.

The message at the end of our Scripture passage is that nothing can separate us from the love of God.

> For I am convinced that neither death, nor life, nor angels, nor rulers, nor things present, nor things to come, nor powers, nor height, nor depth, nor anything else in all creation, will be able to separate us from the love of God in Christ Jesus our Lord. (Romans 8:38–39)

These beautiful and powerful words are at the foundation of my faith. My connection with God is permanent, and nothing can shake that, not even my inability to see or understand that connection.

Read also the full chapter of Romans 8, and check out Psalm 139:7–18.

Questions:

(1) Many consider religion to be a restrictive set of dos and don'ts. However, the author of Romans considered following Jesus as a kind of freedom. What do you think?

(2) In what ways can you resonate with the concept of adoption used in this context? Does the way the author uses it provide support for belonging and inclusion?

(3) What do the words of Romans 8:39 mean to you?

Lesson Three: John 3:1–17
"For God so loved the world . . ."

John 3:16 is a Bible verse that is quoted often, and I like to consider the line in the context of the story. At the beginning of the story, an important leader named Nicodemus meets with Jesus under cover of night. There is a great painting by the African American artist Henry Ossawa Tanner (*Nicodemus*) that depicts the conversation between these two men. We are to assume that this great leader believes in the teachings of Jesus but is hesitant to embrace him publicly. In his talk with Jesus, Nicodemus tries to clarify the idea of being born a second time or "from water and spirit."

In his answer, Jesus rebukes Nicodemus for his confusion and tells him that if he is having trouble receiving what he is hearing now, it will be even harder to accept what is coming up next— meaning Jesus's death and resurrection. Jesus talks about a story from the Old Testament (Numbers 21) when the people upset God, and God sends poisonous serpents to bite and kill everyone. Moses petitions on behalf of the people, and God has Moses hold up a serpent on a stick. Anyone who looks on the serpent, even though they have been bitten, will live. Jesus equates himself with that serpent. Once he has gone through his process of death, resurrection, and ascension, people will be able to look upon him and have eternal life.

John 3:16 sums up the gospel in one sentence: "For God so loved the world that he gave his only Son, so that everyone who believes in him may not perish but may have eternal life." Read together within the context of verses 15 and 17, I believe this presents the best argument for inclusion of all. Jesus is offering himself as a gift that is available to anyone who believes. Additionally, in verse 17, we learn that God did not do all of this to condemn or destroy us but to save us. The sacrifice of Jesus is both as a man who suffers and dies on the cross but also as a divine energy choosing to be human among us. John 3:16 speaks to the motivation of the sacrifice—true love.

Read also 1 Corinthians 13.

Questions:

(1) What is the meaning of eternal life for you? In what ways has that concept changed throughout your life?

(2) Considering the open invitation in John 3:16 to everyone who believes, why do so many Christians focus on exclusion?

(3) What is your connection to the concept of being born again?

A short note about homosexuality in the Bible

In 1984, Phillis Trible wrote a book called *Texts of Terror*, where she discussed various passages and stories from the Bible that have been used to promote sexism and violence against women. In a similar fashion, I would like to list the Scripture passages that have been used to support homophobia and the expulsion of LGBTQ+ Christians from traditional worship spaces. The following is a list of Scripture that I encourage you to read and consider for yourself:

1. Genesis 9:20–27 (the curse of Ham)

2. Genesis 18:16—19:11 (Sodom and Gomorrah)

3. Leviticus 18:22 and 20:13 (holiness codes)

4. Judges 19: 22–30 (the Levite's concubine)

5. Romans 1:26–27 (vice lists)

6. 1 Corinthians 6 and 1 Timothy 1:9–11 (vice lists)

In spite of there being a number of biblical passages that can be interpreted as homosexuality being sin, the argument I hear most often is "God made Adam and Eve and not Adam and Steve!" I also hear people say that the Bible says that marriage is between a man and a woman. The Adam-and-Steve argument seems lazy and is not logically sound but is most certainly harmful to people who want to feel accepted for who they are. And, the Bible has many stories about sexual connections between people. Some people are married. Some men have many wives, as well as mistresses and concubines. There is no simple thing that the Bible says. However, arguing with people is often not helpful, because for them it is an emotional and not a logical or Scripture-based position.

The passages listed above are worth exploring. There are other books that address these issues in a holistic way, arguments around translation and interpretation into which I do not have time to go here.[2] As you read these passages and other parts of the Bible, these are a few things I would like you to consider.

(1) Consider that there is no mention of sexual perversion or homosexuality in the Gospels. As Christians, we believe that the four Gospels—Matthew, Mark, Luke, and John—are the testimony of the birth, life, teachings, death, and resurrection of Jesus Christ. There is no mention of homosexuality as sin in the Gospels. There is an abundance of Scripture on mercy, love, and being nonjudgmental. Therefore, I believe a stronger argument could be made against homophobia than against its victims.

(2) Consider how often the issue of homosexuality is mentioned in the Bible as a whole. The Bible is an agreed-upon canon of books with an array of stories, laws, songs, and poetry to guide

2. Vines, *God and the Gay Christian*; Tonstad, *Queer Theology*; Cheng, *Radical Love*; Perry, *Lord Is My Shepherd*; Bean, *I Was Born This Way*.

us in our understanding of who God is. We cannot ignore that some of the passages are straightforward in the condemnation of same-sex sexual acts; however, there are only seven or eight places where this is mentioned at all in the Bible. Religious leaders who focus on these passages would have you believe that this is what the Bible is about. Also, it seems worth mentioning that homosexuality is not mentioned in the Ten Commandments, nor is it an aspect of the Greatest Commandment, which we have talked about in our journey together. The foundation of our faith is God and God as love. If someone focuses on homosexuality from the pulpit on a regular basis, he is working on his own inner conflicts.

(3) Consider that as society changed, we have changed our view on many other ideas and laws from the Bible. The same passage in Genesis about the curse of Ham was used to justify slavery in America. Most of us have moved on from the notion that to spare the rod is to spoil the child (Proverbs 13:24) and the idea that women should not speak in church (1 Corinthians 14:33–35). We no longer shun children who are born to unwed parents, and most faith traditions allow divorce and marriage after divorce. The passage in Leviticus, for example, is one of hundreds of laws on which we do not focus, and there are many we can no longer accomplish, because our lifestyles have changed so much. We have allowed for our perspectives on other aspects in the Bible to change as society changes. Why is it that so many of us are so intolerant of LGBTQ+ people, when we have become flexible about so many other things?

(4) Read the Bible with suspicion. What is in the Bible, both the translation and the interpretation, has been filtered through human understanding. There is some room to consider that, similar to intolerance in contemporary culture, those who crafted the texts we read in the Bible may have simply been uncomfortable with human sexuality and its diversity. They may have expressed their own biases and attributed them to God.

I would encourage you to read and learn from others so you can make up your own mind. The main point is that the Bible does not support individuals or institutions causing harm to people because of their gender and sexual identities. Nor does the Bible say that God hates anyone. God is love!

Bibliography

"About the Comma." *Normandy Park United Church of Christ*, n.d. https://www.npucc.org/about-the-comma.

Baker-Fletcher, Karen. *Dancing with God: The Trinity from a Womanist Perspective*. St. Louis: Chalice, 2006.

Bass, Ellen, and Laura Davis. *The Courage to Heal: A Guide for Women Survivors of Child Sexual Abuse*. 4th ed. New York: Morrow, 2008.

Bass, Ellen, and Louise Thornton. *I Never Told Anyone: Writings by Women Survivors of Child Sexual Abuse*. 1983. Reprint, New York: Morrow, 1991.

Bean, Carl. *I Was Born This Way: A Gay Preacher's Journey through Gospel Music, Disco Stardom, and a Ministry in Christ*. With David Ritz. New York: Simon & Schuster, 2010.

Brown Douglas, Kelly. *Sexuality and the Black Church: A Womanist Perspective*. Maryknoll, NY: Orbis, 2018.

Carrier, Jim. "Traveling the Civil Rights Trail." *Washington Post*, Aug. 26, 2011. https://www.washingtonpost.com/opinions/traveling-the-civil-rights-trail/2011/08/26/gIQAaVL7gJ_story.html.

Cheng, Patrick S. *Radical Love: An Introduction to Queer Theology*. New York: Seabury, 2011.

Clifford, A. "Feminist Hermeneutics." *Encyclopedia*, n.d. https://www.encyclopedia.com/religion/encyclopedias-almanacs-transcripts-and-maps/feminist-hermeneutics.

Coleman, Monica A. *The Dinah Project: A Handbook for Congregational Response to Sexual Violence*. 2004. Reprint, Eugene, OR: Wipf and Stock, 2010.

Cooper, Ted, Jr. *The Bible in 90 Days*. Grand Rapids: Zondervan, 2005.

Dale, K. A., and Judith L Alpert. "Hiding behind the Cloth: Child Sexual Abuse and the Catholic Church." *Journal of Child Sexual Abuse* 16.3 (2007) 59–74.

"Definition of Ritual Abuse." *First Person Plural*, n.d. https://www.firstpersonplural.org.uk/ritual-abuse/definition-of-ritual-abuse/.

Gil, Eliana. *Outgrowing the Pain: A Book for and about Adults Abused as Children*. New York: Dell, 1988.

Hemingway, Ernest. *A Farewell to Arms*. Scribner Classics. New York: Scribner, 1997.

Heyward, Carter. *The Redemption of God: A Theology of Mutual Relation*. 1982. Reprint, Eugene, OR: Wipf and Stock, 2010.

Johnson, David W., and Jeff VanVonderen. *The Subtle Power of Spiritual Abuse*. Minneapolis: Bethany House, 1991.

Johnson, Timothy J., ed. *Franciscans at Prayer*. Medieval Franciscans 4. Boston: Brill, 2007.

Kinnaman, David, and Gabe Lyons. *UnChristian: What a New Generation Really Thinks about Christianity . . . and Why it Matters*. Grand Rapids: Baker, 2007.

Leibniz, G. W. *Theodicy: Essays on the Goodness of God and the Freedom of Man and the Origin of Evil*. Eugene, OR: Wipf and Stock, 2001.

Lloyd, Rachel. *Girls like Us: Fighting for a World Where Girls Are Not for Sale, an Activist Finds Her Calling and Heals Herself*. New York: HarperCollins, 2011.

McLaren, Peter. *Che Guevara, Paulo Freire, and the Pedagogy of Revolution*. New York: Rowman & Littlefield, 2000.

Montgomery, Brint, et al., eds. *Relational Theology: A Contemporary Introduction*. Eugene, OR: Wipf and Stock, 2012.

Naughty by Nature. "O. P. P." *Naughty by Nature*. New York: Tommy Boy Records, 1991.

Oakley, Lisa, and Kathryn Kinmond. *Breaking the Silence on Spiritual Abuse*. New York: Palgrave Macmillan, 2013.

Pérez-Peña, Richard. "Woman Linked to 1955 Emmett Till Murder Tells Historian Her Claims Were False." *New York Times*, Jan. 1, 2017. https://www.nytimes.com/2017/01/27/us/emmett-till-lynching-carolyn-bryant-donham.html.

Perry, Troy D. *The Lord Is My Shepherd and He Knows I'm Gay: The Autobiography of the Rev. Troy D. Perry, as told to Charles L. Lucas*. Los Angeles: Nash, 1972.

"Research Brief: Religiosity and Suicidality among LGBTQ Youth." *Trevor Project*, Apr. 14, 2020. https://www.thetrevorproject.org/2020/04/14/research-brief-religiosity-and-suicidality-among-lgbtq-youth/.

Schüssler Fiorenza, Elisabeth. *Bread Not Stone: The Challenge of Feminist Biblical Interpretation*. Boston: Beacon, 1984.

Scott, Sara. *The Politics and Experience of Ritual Abuse: Beyond Disbelief*. Philadelphia: Open University, 2001.

Siciliano, Carl. "Religious Rejection and the Crisis of LGBTQ Youth Homelessness." *Impacting Our Future*, n.d. https://www.impactingourfuture.com/lgbtq-empowerment/religious-rejection-and-the-crisis-of-lgbtq-youth-homelessness/.

Thurman, Howard. *Jesus and the Disinherited*. Boston: Beacon, 2012.

Tonstad, Linn Marie. *Queer Theology: Beyond Apologetics.* Eugene, OR: Cascade, 2018.

Trible, Phyllis. *Texts of Terror: Literary-Feminist Readings of Biblical Narratives.* Philadelphia: Fortress, 1984.

Vines, Matthew. *God and the Gay Christian: The Biblical Case in Support of Same-Sex Relationships.* New York: Convergent, 2015.

Volf, Miroslav. *Exclusion and Embrace: A Theological Exploration of Identity, Otherness, and Reconciliation.* Nashville: Abingdon, 1996.

Walker, Alice. *The Color Purple.* New York: Houghton Mifflin Harcourt, 1982.

Wechter, Sharon L. "B'tzelem Elohim, 'In God's Image.'" *Reform Judaism,* n.d. https://reformjudaism.org/learning/torah-study/torah-commentary/btzelem-elohim-gods-image.

"What Is Spiritual Abuse?" *National Domestic Violence Hotline,* n.d. https://www.thehotline.org/resources/what-is-spiritual-abuse/.

Williams, Delores S. *Sisters in the Wilderness: The Challenge of Womanist God-Talk.* Maryknoll, NY: Orbis, 1993.

Young, William P. *The Shack.* Newbury Park, CA: Windblown Media, 2011.